Zone Leader

7 Tactics for Leading in the Zones

By

Dr. Bob Turner

Zone Leader: 7 Tactics for Leading in the Zones

Publisher: Robert Turner

Printed and Bound in the United States of America

Trade Paperback ISBN: 978-1-0879-9339-3

Cover design: Wayne "Batman" Roberts

Contents

Acknowledgement

This book exists because of the combined efforts of many family members and friends. I am thankful for their support, advice, and encouragement during the long hours that went into the finished product.

In researching this book, I met with several leaders from the Armed Forces. I was fortunate to visit with Army Lieutenant Colonel Roger Lewis, who served two deployments in Iraq; Marine Corps Major Michael Castaneda, who also served two deployments in Iraq; retired Army Major General (2 Star) Greg Chaney, who served one deployment in Bosnia and one in Iraq; retired Navy Captain Joseph Torian, who served two deployments in Iraq, one in Asia, and one in Kuwait; retired Navy Vice Admiral Mike Bucchi, who served eight deployments as a fighter pilot in the North Atlantic, Mediterranean, and Indian Ocean; and US Space Force Colonel Eric Dorminey, who served in the Air Force for 29 years, with deployments in the Philippines, Iraq and Afghanistan. These men were an incredible resource and supplied information that is intertwined throughout the analysis of the *Zone Leader*.

To each of these men, thank you. Your contribution to the development of the book overall, specifically the *7 Tactics for Leading in the Zones*, provided insight to illuminate why conflict is so difficult and how a leader can forge on to success even in the face of combat. I appreciate your service to this country and your willingness to guide me in this discussion.

Wayne "Batman" Roberts - thank you for your incredible efforts on the title and graphic work for the cover. I have admired your creativity for many years, and I have appreciated your friendship even longer.

The final draft you read is due to the wonderful work of Reagan Chrisco who took time to edit this writing while studying for finals at Harvard Law School, attending her brother's wedding, moving to Texas, and preparing for her bar exams. Reagan, I cannot thank you enough for your insights, suggestions, and counsel. Your help in completing this book continues to be immeasurable. Thank you!!

I am grateful to Steven Brantz for pushing me to do more and go further than I thought possible. The time spent asking challenging questions and guiding the way forward is one of the reasons you hold this book today. Thank you for being the most positive guy on the planet.

My three children are a blessing beyond the few words in this note. Thank you for always encouraging me to write and taking time to share feedback on how to improve the text, title, and design. You've made me laugh all along the way, and *Zone Leader* is better because of you.

To my wonderful and amazing wife, Sheryl, thank you. Your love and support for more than forty years continue to be a rock for me. I don't want to know life without you. You are amazing, and I am a blessed man because you are in my life. You are the best parts of my past, and you will always be the best parts of my future. Thank you for choosing me. I loved you yesterday, I love you today, and I will love you forever.

I also want to thank each of you for taking time to read this book. No book has value unless it is read and applied. I hope this book possesses that value for you. Thank you.

Bob

Foreword

Life amidst leadership can be overwhelmingly challenging. The stress of leading people, managing projects, raising a family and taking care of oneself can lead to people losing themselves just a bit, or veer off course.

It is natural to allow stress and the daily grind to dull our purpose and passion – especially for those who have lost their roadmap. The cares of the world and pressures to maintain cause some to lose their way.

It doesn't have to be that way. In fact, if you learn to understand where you are at any moment in time, then you can begin to lead yourself and others to reach your goals.

Zone Leader has done a great job laying out a roadmap for all of us to follow. Bob has provided a language to help us learn how to navigate our future. I love what he has done. He has used the common concept of zones to learn how to navigate where we are, why we are there, and how to move forward.

Even more, Bob outlines seven tactics to ensure that we have a practical way of making it through each zone.

I love being challenged to look at my reality – to understand if I am in a comfort zone or not. Additionally, this book will cause you to review what to do when you are in the combat zone, or the danger zone. Ultimately, Bob will help you look at your end zone – the end goal and how to get there.

You will enjoy the many experiences and practical applications to help you become more intentional as a leader and a person.

Get ready to be inspired, to take notes, and begin to live the most intentional life you have ever lived.

- Jeremie Kubicek, best-selling author, global speaker and co-founder of GiANT

PREFACE

With all the books on leadership, why this one? I've read numerous books dealing with multiple aspects of leadership. While many are well-written and applicable for developing and strengthening one's ability to lead, I felt like something was missing. I wanted to know more and explore answers to the questions I was asking.

Through my personal experience and research, I've found that the most overwhelming challenges in leadership involve change. Change is inevitable. Without change death is imminent for any organization. No change means no growth and no growth means failure.

Basically, there are two types of people, those who want change and those who do not. Why? Why do some love it while others hate it? Why are people receptive to change in some areas, but resistant in others? When change is necessary, why is it so difficult to implement? What makes people and organizational culture so resistant to change? The main question to consider as a leader is how can you guide others through the process of change without creating upheaval, division, or destruction?

I realize a quick Google search will highlight thousands of resources that talk about the positive and negative effects of change. Several of these resources have been helpful to me on a personal and professional level. I desire to be a great leader in my home, on my job, and in my community. I have experienced upheaval, division, and destruction when implementing change. I've seen family, friends, and coworkers suffer because of the inability of leaders to guide the process effectively. I knew there had to be a way to address the situation and discover tools to help every leader.

When leaders introduce change into political, civil, corporate, educational, religious, or family structures, resistance will follow. In every arena, change strikes an unusual chord in the minds of many. Leaders are too often ill-equipped to deal with the conflict, fear, and lack of trust that accompanies change. Their inability or lack of confidence in such situations shackles them when trying to reach an appropriate resolution. Leaders need to know how to prepare and respond during such times.

In my pursuit to find answers, I found direction I hope will benefit you, also. The purpose of this book is to help you learn how to lead through times of conflict and the challenges associated with implementing change. As you read through it, think about the application. Read the questions at the end of each chapter and consider how you would answer them for your own leadership and your organization.

Leaders have a responsibility to maintain balance in the face of change. You must not allow present circumstances to alter your ability to lead. Use this resource to guide you through each step, and learn how to better serve your family, organization, or community regardless of the change, conflict, or danger. The more equipped and prepared you are to lead, the more successful your leadership will be in any environment. *The challenges ahead of you can only be measured by the ability inside of you.*

Thank you for picking up this book. You, your family, and your organization will all benefit from your growth.

Bob Turner

Introduction

"Fix your course on a star and you'll navigate any storm."
Leonardo da Vinci

Writing any material on leadership opens one up to scrutiny unlike other topics. Leadership touches every aspect of our lives: political, educational, corporate, religious, and family. The way we view leadership is influenced in part by our understanding of a leader in relationship to these specific arenas. There are also four major leadership styles to consider: autocratic or authoritative leaders, democratic or participative leaders, laissez-faire or free-rein leaders, and paternalistic or familial/relational leaders.[1] These four styles interact and play out in various ways within the five aspects mentioned. Depending on our vantage point as it relates to one area or the other, we define the role of a leader differently.

The scrutiny is real and the challenges unending. On one hand, leadership appears to be one of the most subjective topics. On the other hand, it is universal, because the principles of leadership apply to everyone in all areas of life. Therefore, suggesting an absolute definition or description of successful leadership is a daunting task, difficult at best and impossible at worst. Successful leadership tends to change based on the organization, leadership style, culture, environment, people involved, events surrounding national and international settings, and so much more. Every person has a different concept of what a leader looks like, how a leader acts, where you find leaders today, and why people who demonstrate leadership qualities are often unwilling to take on leadership responsibilities.

The United States—and indeed, the world—is facing a leadership crisis. The Barna Group, an organization that conducts research to provide resources and training for churches, non-profits, businesses, and leaders, surveyed over

15,000 people aged 18-35 and found that more than 80% of participants believed we are facing a leadership crisis.[2] The crisis is not limited to one area, but extends to the home, schools, corporations, government, and the religious community. The consequences are dire: When the right people fail to step up and lead, the wrong ones will. People want to follow someone: The question is, who will they follow?

The COVID-19 pandemic both illuminated and exasperated this leadership crisis. One global pandemic redirected the way our world operates on every level. The increasing variants of the virus created panic in every country. Leaders faced challenges unlike any other time in recent history. Organizational and national leaders constantly dealt with questions related to the lingering effects of COVID-19 and the uncertainty of the future as it relates to these effects.

Everyone was forced into crisis in ways they were not expecting nor prepared to handle. No one could have foreseen the global impact of the virus. Nor could we have known how to prepare for the fallout that resulted. Businesses were forced to shut their doors, some temporarily and some permanently. Because the education system was strained under the pressure of public health concerns and unfamiliar technologies, educational standards suffered. Parents quickly realized the important role educators played in their children's lives. The religious world moved into an arena that challenged its understanding of the assembly, and an online presence redefined how *church* was identified. Political leaders struggled to provide leadership to a world wondering when everything would return to "normal." The world still wrestles with finding answers.

> *As individuals and organizations, we tend to seek out comfort—even at the cost of our long-term success.*

As individuals and organizations, we tend to seek out comfort—even at the cost of our long-term success. Change often causes panic. As a result, leaders fight to maintain a level of comfort and avoid conflict, confrontation, and inconvenience. If life moves along according to the status quo, people often fail to plan for the future, prepare for conflict, or pursue any other course of action. People then become reclusive in their homes, sterile in their spiritual environments, and introverted in their communities and workplaces.

But life doesn't always work out according to our level of comfort. Couples divorce. Cancer destroys. Accidents happen. Parents and children disagree. Employers discipline and fire employees. Indeed, global pandemics take the world by storm. The presence of conflict is unavoidable and can be overwhelming.

While conflict may be handled properly with good preparation, the unexpected is rarely, well…expected. One's inability to gaze into a crystal ball and see the future prevents many leaders from making necessary preparations to handle crises. And when a crisis arises, you have one of three choices. The first choice is to retreat. You do everything in your power to go back to your place of comfort. You desire normalcy, at least as you understand it. The second choice is to face the dangers that accompany stress and anxiety. You experience frustration and fatigue. Your relationships at home and at work are strained. You strive to avoid reality but know at some point you must face these challenges. Ultimately, your third choice is to lead through the crisis and find a place of safety where you can learn about yourself and others. You find new ways to improve the methods of the past and grow. Here, you find respite after enduring the conflict and discover a path forward.

The Evolution of the *Zone Leader*

The evolution of this book has taken place over several years. While refining my presentations for leadership workshops over the last ten years, I have come across many interesting books, articles, blog posts, YouTube clips, visual aids, and charts. One afternoon, I found an image called "The Comfort Zone" by The Wealth Hike. The image depicted four stages of investing: the Comfort Zone, the Fear Zone, the Learning Zone, and the Growth Zone.[3] Each zone was identified by specific characteristics. As I examined the image, I was struck by the relationship between these zones and what I considered to be concepts of successful leadership. This image inspired me to develop a philosophy on what zones leaders often find themselves in and how leaders can push through them to reach real success.

I began presenting the material to test out the philosophy at leadership events. On one occasion, a friend of mine attended one of these workshops. Later, as we discussed the presentation, he mentioned that I was missing a zone—what he referred to as the "Success Zone." I agreed, so I started the process of identifying characteristics of the Success Zone for my presentation. A few months later, while making a similar presentation for a group in Lubbock, Texas, I discussed the evolution of these zones to include my friend's suggestion. Immediately after the presentation, a gentleman told me about a leadership presentation he had heard when he was younger. The presenter referred to what he called the "Danger Zone." My mind started racing, and I quickly began developing another zone for my presentation.

Almost one month later, I was running with a friend in Kentucky, where I participated in a Leadership Retreat. During our run, I shared the evolution of these zones and how humorous the process was for me as they developed. I told him I felt like there was one zone missing and I couldn't figure out what it was…at least not yet. As we continued to run and talk about the various elements of the zones, I had a revelation: the "Practice Zone." This was the missing piece, which rounded out

4

the chart, or so I thought. Others suggested additional zones like the "Discovery Zone" and a "Safety Zone." You understand my dilemma. The chart illustrates my *initial* thought process for developing the zones. The project, however, needed work to provide a more simplified approach to leading through each zone.

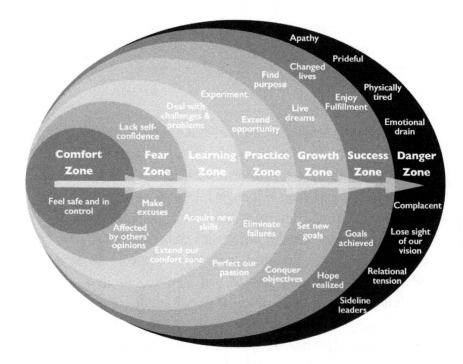

The philosophy was not complete. One night, I woke up about 3 AM and could not stop thinking about the material and how I wanted to approach it. I had just finished reading Bob Goff's book *Dream Big*,[4] a book that challenges every person to live an extraordinary life, to become the best version of themselves. Several ideas kept floating around in my mind. I knew there had to be more, something I was missing, something extraordinary. The longer I laid in the bed, the more I kept mulling over the conflict leaders face. That is when I developed the Combat Zone. From here, I knew that with the onslaught of conflict there had to be a way to recover, a place to celebrate, and so the End Zone rounded out the concept of zone leadership. However, the final product needed to be further refined.

Before I explore the zones in their completed form, let me explain the final step. The philosophy presented here evolved through multiple presentations and with the counsel of good friends and fellow leaders. As I worked out the characteristics of the zones, as you can see on the previous page, the image looked more like a solar system than a leadership resource and it became more complicated to explain. This is when I had the opportunity to sit down with Jeremie Kubicek, executive chairman and co-founder of GiANT Worldwide and GiANT TV. The collaboration led to how I could develop the material into a book, a path to simplify the process, the proper number of zones, and a plan to connect an application for leadership. My discussions with Jeremie changed the trajectory of this book and its application. In the end, I synthesized the philosophy into four major zones that every leader encounters: the Comfort Zone, the Combat Zone, the Danger Zone, and the End Zone.

Finding Your Zone

What does all this mean for you? Where do you fit in these leadership zones? Most leaders aspire to reach the greatest level of success, but to reach this point of success, you must consider a few key questions. First, what does success look like for you? The only way to know if you succeeded is to define the ultimate goal. Second, do you know which zone you are in currently? Without an awareness of your current situation, all the wishing in the world for success is futile. Third, depending on your current leadership zone, what are you doing to move past your present situation to achieve success? Success requires discipline and hard work, and without a vision, established goals and plans, you will struggle to move past your current reality. Fourth, what are you willing or unwilling to do to reach that success? The way you answer this question is critical and your answer speaks volumes about your core values, your knowledge of leadership and the current crisis, your self-awareness of strengths and weaknesses, the abilities of those with whom you work, and your desire to move into a new reality.

Use this opportunity to review your progress, not only as it relates to organizational goals but also in relationship to your ability to follow through on commitments to yourself and your values. Do you have enough self-respect to not cross the line on what you said you would or would not do? Knowing your response often determines the difference between real success and failure.

Let me share my son's experience from early in his career as a leader. He learned a critical lesson about values, specifically, how to respond when you tell yourself what you will not do. In his words, "I worked hard to put systems in place at the plant (especially on the front end of my time as plant manager) that would allow me to have an appropriate work/life balance."

Unfortunately, several unexpected issues arose within the organization, as the company was acquired by a large international investment firm, and it soon became crunch time. Because he didn't stand up for himself demanding the needed and deserved support, he worked longer and harder than necessary, attempting to *power through* until the issues were resolved. For months he unknowingly betrayed the values and systems he initially established, denying his self-worth. Eventually, he resented himself, his job, and those around him. It's a vicious cycle that is often fueled by a strange mixture of pride and insecurity. These situations often create the perfect storm of frustration that, if ignored, almost always leads to failure.

Situations of this nature challenge most leaders, especially early in their leadership journey. Sadly, many do not learn and grow as a leader, and the consequences are costly. Thankfully, for my son, the situation made him a stronger leader and he has gone on to lead in larger organizations.

Let me summarize the zones in a more concise way as we begin the journey. As the image depicts, the Comfort Zone is a place where everyone is comfortable.

You can say things are just average. The status quo rules. At times, you might feel bored, but you are comfortable. The major characteristic of this zone is normalcy because there is a sense of safety and control. In other words, people want a level of comfort, a place of familiarity, where life is predictable, and they can control what goes on around them. Perhaps the worst part of this zone is the lack of appropriate risk involved, thus limiting the growth of the individual and organization.

Leading people out of the Comfort Zone is not an easy task. Once someone is comfortable with the status quo, roots grow deep, like a mighty oak tree. It takes a strong leader to lead an organization through this zone, because once movement begins, so does resistance. Regretfully, too many individuals and organizations find themselves in this zone, and often uncertain as to the future because the change required to move forward makes them uncomfortable.

The Combat Zone is a place where conflict develops from the resistance created by change. Change moves us out of our Comfort Zone, and it creates many challenges for you as a leader. When you lead, you must prepare for conflict. The following image highlights two major types of conflict characteristic of the Combat Zone: forced and initiated.

Forced conflict arises when you least expect it. You are unprepared, and when unprepared, you are impaired as a leader. You struggle with how to communicate, operate, and negotiate successfully. However, initiated conflict happens with a level of expectation, because you prepare and communicate upcoming changes to those affected by them. Initiated conflict minimizes resistance. When prepared, you reorganize, tighten the budget, plan, and think tactically, or rethink how you communicate, operate, and negotiate more successfully.

As I mentioned, moving out of the Comfort Zone usually occurs when change is introduced, and when you implement change, conflict follows. The conflict experienced in the Combat Zone also opens the door to fear: fear associated with insecurity, uncertainty, and the unknown. During these times, you must remain focused on the organization's vision. If not handled correctly, a lack of trust develops, and followers become skeptical of your leadership creating greater challenges. You must understand the critical nature of continually improving your leadership ability to encourage forward movement. The success of any organization rests on its leaders' ability to resolve conflict, minimizing the resistance. However, if the conflict is great enough, leaders find it easy to drift back into the Comfort Zone, as the visual indicates.

As you lead through one of the most challenging zones, what will be required of you? Courage and character. Your response as a leader when facing the conflict and fear experienced in the Combat Zone determines your direction through this zone. The courage demonstrated in making decisions under pressure and the strength of your character will instill confidence in those who follow your lead. While it may seem easy to go back into the Comfort Zone, something more threatening exists: the potential of entering the Danger Zone.

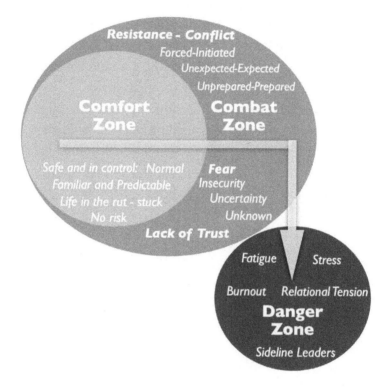

The Danger Zone represents the place where you often find yourself as a result of being unprepared. The Danger Zone challenges the core of your leadership, primarily because you are tired or overwhelmed. The stress you experience while leading through the Combat Zone produces a level of frustration that pushes you to react rashly instead of acting like a healthy leader. You will battle against pride and arrogance. You will experience difficulties in your relationships, which often creates a dysfunctional organization. Leading in the Danger Zone requires you to stop and re-evaluate your priorities, vision, mission, goals, and the organization's greater good.

The Danger Zone can raise its ugly head at any time in the journey, and it is characterized by immense amounts of stress, fatigue, burnout, relational tension, and what I refer to as sideline leadership. There is never a time where danger does not exist. You must guard against the defeating powers that threaten your leadership and lurk around every corner. Never get complacent. Do not lose sight of the vision. Avoid the temptation to drift back into the Comfort Zone. Fight against the demons of pride and arrogance. Hold on with all your might. The journey will not be easy, but you must keep in mind the value of achieving each step toward the reward that awaits around the next bend in the road—the End Zone.

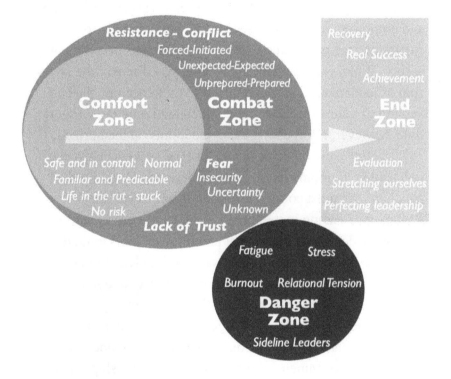

The End Zone represents a place of recovery. Here, you celebrate victory and reflect on the journey to help build confidence and further prepare for future challenges. When you are prepared, successfully moving through the Combat Zone, you reach a place where you stretch yourself and learn. While the End Zone is not the end of the journey, it is a point of rest, recovering from the battles of conflict, discovering who you are as a leader, evaluating, finding ways to fine tune your leadership, and preparing for the next adventure. Once you arrive, you will love and value the sense of achievement.

The beauty of this zone is more than just evaluating where you've been, where you are, and where you want to go. In the End Zone, you begin to practice what you have learned and experiment with ways to perfect your skills. As a leader, you realize as others have said before, "Success is not final; failure is not fatal." You constantly seek a vision that inspires and empowers others to be successful, and you long to experience the power and excitement of dreams becoming a reality. When you reach the End Zone, you discover the sweet spot of leadership. This space allows you to become the best version of yourself. The excitement created only lasts a short time, however, as repeating the cycle looms on the horizon.

How can you achieve this level of success? How can you lead your organization through these zones? As I will conclude, the most concise approach is what I call the "7 Tactics for Leading in the Zones." The tactics presented in this book provide you with practical and relevant tools to guide you in leading through the turbulent waters of leadership in our current culture. However, these tools will offer much more than just a guide to leading an organization. The strategy will help anyone lead through the challenges encountered when introducing change on a personal level, in your home, within your work environment, and even where you worship. This guide has been developed, in part, to help you effectively evaluate your leadership by raising an awareness of your zone and prescribing a plan for how to move forward.

For perspective, the visual is a view of the final product I call *The Zones of Leadership.*

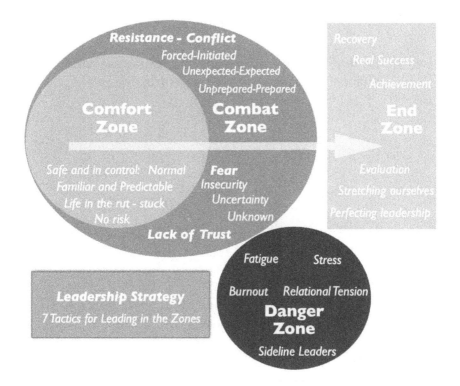

The characteristics of each zone will be discussed in the following pages, along with a plan for leading through that zone. Ultimately, the seven tactics identified in this book will equip you with the tools for successful leadership in all areas of life. As you read each chapter, consider where you are as a leader and how you can move past your current zone to lead your organization to greater success. I hope to help you develop the skills necessary to forge ahead toward the End Zone. I invite you to dive into each chapter with an honest evaluation of your leadership and learn how to lead your organization successfully.

Each chapter concludes with a list of questions designed to challenge the way you think about your leadership and the leadership of your organization. Reflect on them, consider where you are, and how you can use your answers to lead through the Zones. Indeed, introspection is a key element of successful leadership.

In The Zone

1. Prior to taking your first step on this journey, take a moment to write down your organization's:

   a. Vision

   b. Mission

   c. Values

2. Which of these three is most important to you as a leader and your organization? Why?

3. As you begin reviewing the Zones, where do you currently see yourself as a leader? Your organization?

4. Describe your approach to handling change as a leader.

5. At this point in time, write out your plan for moving from where you are to where you want to be as a leader and for your organization?

Chapter One

The Comfort Zone

"The comfort zone is the great enemy to creativity; moving beyond it necessitates intuition, which in turn configures new perspectives and conquers fears."
Dan Stevens

Routine is the name of the game for me. I have a daily routine that rarely changes. When it does change, things do not seem to function as well. For example, something as small as changing our clocks to daylight saving time can throw my routine off balance. It may not seem like much, but a one-hour time-change is usually enough to throw my sleeping routine off for an entire week.

We can thank Benjamin Franklin for introducing this practice in 1784. The proposal was intended to save money by reducing the need to use candles in the evenings. For more than 238 years this practice has continued, even though the advent of modern electricity has completely done away with the reason it first started. Change is hard, especially when we are comfortable with a practice that has been in place for more than two centuries. Complacency and the fear of change can lead to practices that inconvenience everyone and help no one.

The example illustrates how easily things can become stagnant, even amid changing circumstances. This is true in our personal lives and in corporate settings. Change is happening all around us: It occurs on a second-by-second basis. However, you may discover that many of your daily routines are based on years if not decades of practice. Even amid constant change, there is still so much in life that remains stagnant. Why is this so? Perhaps it is because complacency, stagnancy, and fear of change provide building blocks to our comfort zone.

I love my comfort zone. Once I developed my routines and became comfortable with them, I also became quite resistant to change. The challenge with this approach to life or business is the potential of becoming complacent and stagnant, even when circumstances change all around us.

> *When we settle for less than what we can achieve if pushed a little beyond our comfort level, growth is stymied.*

When we settle for less than what we can achieve if pushed a little beyond our comfort level, growth is stymied.

What Is the Comfort Zone?

The Comfort Zone is best described by a fixed mindset i.e., it is highly resistant to change. Leaders become comfortable with the status quo. Organizations may *desire* growth and expansion. However, it's more like an empty wish, because of the unwillingness to change. Change disrupts the level of comfort that exists, and any effort is viewed as too much work, or worthless. Everything remains the same.

As I will discuss in this chapter, the Comfort Zone is characterized by being comfortable, digging a rut and staying in it, a false sense of security and success, familiarity and predictability, and a lack of risk. The Comfort Zone may feel safe, but in reality, it is a dangerous zone for a leader: It stifles innovation and growth, causing leaders to abandon the best versions of themselves in a world where quality leadership is desperately needed.

It's Comfortable

The Comfort Zone is what it sounds like— it's comfortable. When things work well, it is easy to get comfortable and stop looking for ways to improve. The phrase, "if it ain't broke, don't fix it" generally describes the thought process. Many of us enjoy being in control, having a regular routine, avoiding confrontation, and dodging risk.

As an interesting case-study to illustrate the danger of becoming too comfortable, let's examine the fall of Borders bookstore. Advances in technology and online shopping have strained the success of brick-and-mortar retailers throughout the country for more than twenty years. We continue to witness the decline of retailers that were once a mainstay for our shopping needs. Stores like Montgomery Wards, Sears, Toys-R-Us, and Sports Authority were popular for retail shoppers, but they were unable to keep up with the changing trends of American consumers. Borders bookstore was a popular retail chain that also suffered the same consequences.

The first Borders store opened in 1971 in Ann Arbor, Michigan. Over the twenty-five years that followed, Borders became a national chain that rivaled its biggest competitor, Barnes and Noble. However, technological changes and advances in online sales took a toll on Borders' profit margins. Their inability to respond to these changes quickly led to the decline in sales and insurmountable debt until they filed bankruptcy and liquidated the company in 2011.

I could discuss numerous reasons why Borders no longer exists, just as others have suggested: delay in using online technology, delay in the use of e-books, relying on brick-and-mortar retail, massive debt, bad leadership, marketing, and more. But each of these factors fall within a larger problem: Borders stayed in the Comfort Zone. While attempts to make changes did occur, these attempts came too late. The company outsourced their online market instead of creating their own. They were comfortable with the profits connected to their physical presence. As one source identified, "Borders was the only major book retailer that was almost completely dependent on people getting in their car, going to their store, and purchasing a physical book."[5] The result outlined the demise of the company within a short time.

Borders is only one of several corporations that suffered the same fate and often for the same reasons. While the short-term desire for comfort dominates, the long-term cost of remaining in the Comfort Zone can result in a death blow to any organization. If you don't recognize the characteristics of the Comfort Zone and take steps to avoid or get out of it, the consequences are inescapable.

A friend of mine says it this way, "Individuals and organizations willing to live in the Comfort Zone are unwilling to understand the nature of change. This means that the amount of change will many times build up to catastrophic levels later in life versus allowing incremental change to occur."

People desire comfort. Rarely do leaders seek and enjoy change, conflict, or controversy. While no leader wants to deal with these challenges, avoiding them often promotes staying in the Comfort Zone. Depending on the industry (retail vs defense), this can be referred to as chaos. Leaders may not look for conflict, but they can't sit still either. In this Zone, however, no one innovates. No one grows. Things simply stay the same— even if another course would be better. As time passes, the rut created by the Comfort Zone only grows deeper, making it that much more difficult to claw your way out.

Digging a Rut and Staying in It

Growing up in rural Missouri and Arkansas led me down many dirt roads. If you found yourself on a dirt road, you were probably there intentionally—going to visit friends, heading to the local swimming hole, or taking a shortcut between paved roads. Rural communities employed county road crews tasked with grading the roads to make them passable.

This was an important task, because whenever it rained, many of these roads became so rough they were difficult or even impossible to drive on safely. When people drove on these roads after a big rain, their tires often created deep ruts in the mud. Once hardened by the sun, they were difficult to escape. If not proceeding carefully, a driver could over-steer and drive into a ditch, a tree, a creek, or oncoming traffic. It takes strength to steer a vehicle out of the rut, because riding in it is comfortable and forcing the tires over its barriers takes power. In other words, it requires effort and risk.

The ruts we form by staying in the Comfort Zone make it difficult to dig our way out. I remember a friend who told me, "The rut becomes the path of least resistance and even if you want to steer the car in a different direction, without persistent and firm steering, the car always finds itself back in the rut. Likewise in personal and organizational ruts, the only way to get out of them (i.e., change) is with consistent and persistent pressure. Without the effort of both, you will always find yourself back in the rut." In our everyday lives, we build our routines. And while these routines make us feel comfortable, they can also have more dangerous effects: They can dig us deeper into our routines making it harder to change course. The ripple effect impacts those we lead, and organizational challenges grow.

As I admitted before, I love my routines. I enjoy getting up at the same time each morning, spending time in prayer and reading, exercising, enjoying the same breakfast, eating lunch and supper at the same time each day, and going to bed at the same time each night. The older I get, and the longer I hold on to these daily practices, the more miserable I am when something obstructs my routine. Maybe these routines are fine when it comes to my breakfast of choice or daily exercise, but they can hold me back when circumstances necessitate a change.

Getting and staying in a rut not only happens to us individually, but it also occurs on the organizational level. This happens because contented leaders can influence the entire organization to become complacent and act too slowly to market changes, just as I mentioned with Borders bookstore. What creates this rut mentality and what keeps people in it? Let's explore a few possibilities.

The past. Past failures, past successes, past relationships, past experiences, and past traditions can all contribute to stagnation. Intellectually, you know that you can't go back and change the past but knowing that and getting out of the rut created by the past are two different things completely. On the one hand, it's natural to be shaped by the past: Your very identity is directly connected to past experiences. Your mental and emotional health are shaped by your past. Your ability to read, think critically, reason logically, assess situations, and act on those assessments come from your past. But on the other hand, your past can hold you back from creating a different future. I am not suggesting that the past be abandoned or that the influences of the past be forgotten. What I am saying is that you must not remain *beholden* to the past, allowing it to hinder you from moving forward. Colonel Eric Dorminey said it this way, "The past teaches lessons and can help assess the impact of what just happened but getting fixated on it only leads to disaster. The past can inform the path through recognition of how you got here but the past is ineffective at advancing you down the path."

Preconceived ideas. Related to your past experiences, preconceived ideas also cause the same. Generally, your morals, ethics, religious beliefs, concept of family, and life strategy are developed through preconceived notions. Your ideas can be right, or they can be wrong. Often, preconceived ideas become so engrained that we cannot accept anything that contradicts them. We perceive any threat to our preconceived notions as a challenge to our very identity. It becomes difficult to set those preconceived ideas aside to learn something new. Has anyone ever asked you to "keep an open mind"? This expression is another way of asking you to put aside your preconceived ideas and listen to another perspective. When we fail to practice mental flexibility—or in other words, to keep an open mind—we allow our preconceived ideas to pull us into a rut and keep us there.

> *When we fail to practice mental flexibility—or in other words, to keep an open mind—we allow our preconceived ideas to pull us into a rut and keep us there.*

Dreadmill Syndrome. There is a phenomenon in the running community that I like to call the "Dreadmill Syndrome." Many runners enjoy putting in their mileage on outdoor paths and become accustomed to the fresh air and scenery nature provides. The last place they want to run is on a treadmill. In fact, when running outdoors is not an option, many would rather not run at all—they would do anything to avoid the "dreadmill." Why do they dread the treadmill so much? To put it simply, they feel like they aren't getting anywhere. Even though they exercise their legs, each step feels futile as they stare at the same screen, watching the seconds clip by and the distance slowly add up. For some, it is more tiring to run on a treadmill than to run outdoors, surrounded by beauty and breathing in the fresh air.

Sadly, leaders will often get trapped in the proverbial dreadmill mindset. They make the effort and desire to move ahead. However, the Comfort Zone mindset usually prevails, and the essential steps required to truly move forward end up on the back burner. You will find that you are busy, working, and moving but never making progress. One potential cause is the conflation of being busy with achievement. The two concepts are not equal. As Denzel Washington put it in a Dillard University commencement address, "Do not confuse movement with progress, because you can run in place and never get anywhere."[6] Once you're in the rut, the dreadmill keeps you there: You keep moving, but never really get anywhere.

Stress and anxiety. While it may seem paradoxical, the characteristics of the Comfort Zone can sometimes be the products of stress and anxiety. There seems to be plenty of stress and anxiety to go around. Even our continuous efforts to maintain the status quo of the Comfort Zone can cause stress and anxiety. When leaders and organizations notice changes in the world around them, the potential influence raises concerns. To prevent the influence of these changes—right or wrong— and remain in a comfortable place, leaders often spend their time and energy constantly focused on maintaining the current status. The deeper the rut, the more stress experienced in trying to maintain it. To keep change at bay, we buckle under the pressure to maintain our present form and function. This results in more stress, which often leads us down a path of greater anxiety, all because the desire to remain comfortable is so pressing.

Comparative living. Closely associated with stress and anxiety is the characteristic of comparative living. The constant barrage of what others do and how they look at what we do consumes us. The stress and anxiety associated with comparative living deepens the rut mentality, because you constantly compare your leadership to someone else and miss reaching your own potential as a leader. Learning from the leadership acumen of others can be vital to improving your own abilities to lead. However, when you find yourself falling short because you can never quite achieve what others have achieved, stress and anxiety increase to debilitating levels.

In his book, *T.R.I.A.L.S.,* Chase Turner beautifully explores how comparative living raises anxiety.[7] While stress is inevitable, he suggests you can prevent stress from leading to anxiety by learning how to properly define what is normal and avoid the comparative living mindset. In the Comfort Zone, leaders and organizations constantly compare what they do with others around them. The tendency is to judge everyone else by your own current standard of thinking and operating. The cycle created by this lifestyle not only leads to greater stress and anxiety, but it also increases friction in relationships.

Fatigue. At various times in life, everyone gets tired. Fatigue comes in the form of mental duress, emotional depletion, physical strain, or spiritual exhaustion. Various levels of fatigue will rob you of energy and hinder your ability to concentrate. One fascinating feature of fatigue is that you do not have to do anything different, and yet you still feel tired all the time. After all, how much effort does it take to maintain your level of comfort and prevent change? Fatigue can result from or create a rut—but regardless of which comes first, fatigue can certainly *keep you* in it. Thankfully, fatigue can be prevented and overcome with proper rest.

Lack of direction. Without vision, all we have to guide us is our comfort level. When leaders and organizations do not know who they want to become, they have no idea how to get anywhere. They simply stay the course of immobility. For example, leaders have convinced themselves that to stay far away from a conservative or progressive influence, they must go in the opposite direction. Sadly, they cannot see they have gone too far in the opposite direction and created as many or more problems. Why is it so difficult to have balance and prevent going from one extreme to the other? The only way to achieve balance is with *vision*: knowing the direction ahead and intentionally steering the organization in that direction.

There are likely other influences that dig us into a rut or keep us there. Regardless of its source, staying in it is debilitating, and can be destructive. A friend of mine once told me, "A rut walked in long enough becomes a grave." This explains why it is a key characteristic of the Comfort Zone.

A False Sense of Security and Success

Another key feature of the Comfort Zone—and perhaps the most dangerous—is a false sense of security and success. This false sense is the natural consequence of staying in the rut: Once you justify who and where you are, it becomes increasingly difficult to see the need for change. This is dangerous for three reasons.

First, as the heading indicates, a *false* sense of security and success indicates you believe something that does not really exist. Consider someone who sees a post on social media, and without investigating the validity of the post, shares it. Because the post aligns with their belief system, they begin telling others of this new-found "truth," which is actually false. They *feel* validated, even though it is rooted in something that isn't true. Anytime we are convinced something exists when it does not, we create a false sense of understanding, security, stability, and hope. As a leader, it is critical to remember that when you focus on maintaining the status quo and promoting life in the Comfort Zone, you create a *false* sense of security and success. Are you willing to carefully examine what you do and why you do it and make needed changes to move beyond the Comfort Zone?

Second, security is vital to every person and every organization, and believing in *false* security prevents us from gaining *true* security. Several years ago, I had the privilege of developing a friendship with a wonderful couple. Later, I learned that they struggled in their marriage and the primary reason involved this concept of security. His concept of security was far different than hers. He relished in the idea of a simple life: living off the land, staying in the great outdoors, roughing it, taking one day at a time, traveling, not worrying about the future, and allowing the love they had for one another to direct them. However, she desired job security for both of them, a home to call her own, watching children grow up and get married, and one day enjoying grandchildren. Since they had different ideas about the nature of security, they struggled to feel secure at the same time. One's security was the other's chaos. As you can guess, this led to conflict.

As this example demonstrates, everyone has their own sense of security and what provides security for them. This is true for organizations as well. Insecurity is usually the result of uncertainty and instability. Security is produced by something concrete, often characterized by financial stability, a place to live, a vision for the future, a safe environment, established goals and plans, etc. While people may have different measures of security, one truth remains constant: They look to leaders to provide it. When their leaders provide security, they feel a certain level of confidence and peace. But when those same leaders fail to provide this need, they look for someone else to lead them. This is why false security is so dangerous: It sets the leader and those being led up for failure. When leaders stay in the Comfort Zone, they lead constituents down the wrong path by allowing them to *feel* secure without the proper foundation for *true* security.

Third, regardless of how success is defined, everyone desires to be successful. Like false security prevents the realization of true security, a false sense of success prevents the realization of true success. Defining success is subjective to the individual and organization. For some, success is related to profit, expansion, or other tangible ideas that can be measured in numbers. For others, success is more about quality than quantity. Becoming a better husband, wife, father, mother, brother, sister, friend, neighbor, citizen, employer,

> "Success is having those who know you best respect you the most." John Maxwell

or employee can be measures of success. Those who follow this vision of success might agree with John Maxwell's statement that "success is having those who know you best respect you the most."[8]

A false sense of security and success can emerge when we allow our goals to slowly drift away. With all the advances in technology, education, medicine, and science, why are families more dysfunctional today than years past? Why do some companies excel, and others fail? Is it possible that we have mis-defined success? Have we allowed ourselves to *believe* we are succeeding while slowly allowing our leadership to disintegrate, our families to become less involved in matters of greater importance, and our society to become more obsessed with self-centeredness? When our organizations struggle, a false sense of security and success is at least worth considering.

Familiarity and Predictability

Familiarity and predictability are two sides of the same coin when characterizing the Comfort Zone. Familiarity describes a place where form and function are thoroughly known and common. There is a sense of mastery. Predictability follows because the familiarity of form and function secures those things never change; thus, they are predictable. You become so comfortable with how well you perform these functions that the thought of change is terrifying. They are done the same way as they were yesterday, the day before, and for decades or even centuries of time.

In his article "Why Good Companies Go Bad," Donald Sull refers to this condition as *active inertia*. He writes, "Active inertia is an organization's tendency to follow established patterns of behavior—even in response to dramatic environmental shifts. Stuck in the modes of thinking and working that brought success in the past, market leaders simply accelerate all their tried-and-true activities. In trying to dig themselves out of a hole, they just deepen it."[9] Why do these organizations perpetuate this pattern? Because it is familiar and predictable.

Among many organizations that prolong active inertia, the world of religion tops the list. Many religious organizations live within the familiarity of form and function. The purpose ensures that regardless of the location, congregants know exactly what to expect because assemblies are conducted the same way every week. Predictability entered the picture when the traditions established in previous generations became entrenched in the practices of succeeding generations. Leaders then safeguarded those practices to prevent change.

While I understand the intent and design of such familiarity and predictability, a problem arises when these two components keep you in the Comfort Zone and prevent growth. Leaders do well to know that many traditional practices were put in place because of specific cultural needs that existed during a particular time in the organization's history. However, as cultural changes occur from one generation to another, so do the needs. Attempts to meet these new needs with archaic practices associated with previous traditions are often met with resistance. The primary reason is because such practices lack relevance for the current reality. The results handcuff leaders and organizations to the past in ways that not only prevent change, but also growth.

One of the main reasons the Comfort Zone is so comfortable is because it is a familiar place of predictability. We know what to expect because we've done it before. "We've always done it this way" becomes the mantra for maintaining the current standard of operation. Yet, these six words produce a slow and painful death for any leader and organization.

Risk Averse

The Comfort Zone involves actively avoiding the risk associated with change—it embodies the phrase, "better safe than sorry." However, what many leaders do not understand is that actively avoiding risk is a risk that often results in disaster. How many opportunities have been lost because someone played it safe and was unwilling to take a risk? This is not to say that we should take every risk that presents itself but playing it safe does not promote healthy growth and development either. Sadly, when you step into the arena of risk-taking, you start feeling extremely uncomfortable. In some ways, those feelings may be justified, but great leadership never develops from avoiding risk altogether. Neale Walsch once said, "Life begins at the end of your comfort zone. So, if you're feeling uncomfortable right now, know that the change taking place in your life is a beginning, not an ending."[10] Allowing your life to begin at the end of your Comfort Zone requires you to understand the importance of taking appropriate risks.

Risk-taking is a risky business. Leaders not only need to learn how to take appropriate risks, but they must also train others to do the same, so they have a better chance to develop. My wife and I learned this when our children were infants. We watched them learn how to crawl, then walk, and then run. Now, more than forty years later, we watch our grandchildren do the same. We often recount how fearless our children appeared to be. My wife and I watched with great excitement as each of our kids took their first step. As they took those steps, we encouraged them to take a risk and push themselves beyond crawling. If we only allowed our children to crawl, keeping them safe from the bumps and bruises that accompany those falls when they learned to walk and run, what would have happened to them mentally and physically? Obviously, this would stunt their growth tremendously. I've wondered if it is not the parents' expression of fear that creates a fearful mindset in children, long before they develop it on their own. There are risks involved as children grow up, and when they are constantly held back it hinders them from reaching their full potential. If they never take risks, they fail to mature biologically, physiologically, or psychologically.

Perhaps it is obvious, but we did *not* let our children learn to take their first steps by setting them at the top of the stairs without precautionary measures. There is a difference in calculated risk-taking and throwing caution to the wind.

As a leader, if you hold back your organization by never taking risks, then the Comfort Zone is all you will get. You will never learn the important skill of assessing risk, and your organization will never reach its full potential. No faith is required to remain in the Comfort Zone. It is business as usual. You know what to do and you do it because that is the only way you know, and you do it well. You have mastered the art of form and function. Since others may have previously established the Comfort Zone, you see no need to challenge yourself by expanding your knowledge base and introduce change. The long-term effects are inhibitive and destructive.

How Can You Escape the Comfort Zone?

One of the greatest challenges of the Comfort Zone is the issue of control. After all, leaders are perceived as having control. They discover the vision, establish goals, implement plans, make all the decisions, and hold everyone accountable for the work that needs to be done. But in the Comfort Zone, you may find yourself with a different purpose when it comes to control: The control you exercise is primarily focused on maintenance. You exert all your energy trying to maintain the status quo.

As a result, organizations neglect leadership training and instead focus solely on job training. If your goal is to remain in the Comfort Zone, you don't really need to invest in making people better *leaders*; instead, you'll focus on teaching them how to maintain the status quo. The result stifles growth. As the aforementioned survey conducted by the Barna Group

> *If your goal is to remain in the Comfort Zone, you don't really need to invest in making people better **leaders**; instead, you'll focus on teaching them how to maintain the status quo. The result stifles growth.*

reveals, a large percentage of 18–35-year-olds believe that the reason we have a leadership crisis is because older leaders do not allow younger leaders to actually lead.[11] What an indictment! If we want our organizations to experience long-term success, something must change. Why? One reason is because "comfort and growth do not coexist."[12]

Giving up control is one of the hardest suggestions to implement. Our works-based culture has contributed to the do-it-yourself or do-it-on-your-own way of thinking. There are certainly people in my life who encouraged this mindset in me, but the bottom line is that no one is responsible for it except me. Any time I begin thinking I can make it on my own, I know I am moving in the wrong direction. Although everyone is influenced to some degree by the individualistic thinking of our culture, in the end, success only comes when this journey through life is lived out in community, helping others.

Some of my favorite books and articles on leadership illustrate the multiplication effect of developing leaders who reproduce leaders. For example, Jeremie Kubicek and Steve Cockram's book, *100x Leader,* highlights the success of leaders who reach their potential by developing others to lead.[13] The greatest success enjoyed by any organization occurs through effective implementation of succession planning—leaders developing leaders. As John Maxwell so accurately assesses, "To add growth, lead followers—to multiply, lead leaders."[14]

The battle at hand involves answering a critical question, "How do we get out of the Comfort Zone and move forward?" The journey ahead presents many challenges. The next Zone introduces conflict and fear—the kind of conflict and fear that often incapacitates people and drives them back to the Comfort Zone. As a result, the answer to the question requires moving into areas that are unknown and, frankly, scary. I will suggest several steps. You do not necessarily need to take every suggestion, but I encourage you to take a few minutes to look through them and use the suggestions that are helpful to you. Hopefully, you are convicted enough to take steps to move out of your Comfort Zone into greater possibilities.

Do a Reality Check

Getting out of the Comfort Zone requires realizing that you're in it. This can be difficult because many people do not enjoy looking in the mirror of introspect. Once, while counting down the recommended twenty seconds as I washed my hands, I found myself looking in the mirror. I began to look into my eyes, not to see if there was anything in them or to examine the dark circles under them, but to really look at *myself*—to examine my soul. I began to ask all sorts of questions. Who am I, really? Have I challenged myself to leave points of comfort to grow? Am I helping others reach their potential? What do I intend to do with the time I have left on earth? How can I grow further to understand my life's purpose more deeply? I quickly thought about the events that have shaped who I am and where I am today. How can I build something greater for the future?

These questions are difficult, but they enable us to diagnose our limitations and forge a path forward. When was the last time you sat down and honestly questioned whether you are in the Comfort Zone? Perhaps your own reality check looks different than mine, but until you can honestly sit down and consider these questions, it will be difficult to push beyond comfort.

Without examination, your natural tendency is to seek comfort. This examination, however, is not a one-time look into your inner self. You must continue to examine your life and leadership. Introspection is the linchpin for growth. The moment you get comfortable, you should be uncomfortable, because something isn't right. As I will explore in the chapter on the Danger Zone, the point of comfort is also a point of danger, and you must move beyond it, stretching yourself to something bigger and better. You need a reality check. Take the initiative to ask yourself difficult questions and have the courage to answer them honestly.

> *The moment you get comfortable, you should be uncomfortable, because something isn't right.*

Challenge the Rut

If you know what characterizes the rut, you have the tools to begin challenging it. Just as a driver must use strength and caution, with a bit of risk, to navigate their vehicle out of those tracks, a leader can only get out of the Comfort Zone by making the changes needed to move the organization out of it.

I was privileged to lead an international program based out of Denver for eight years. During this time, I learned about international travel, culture, and 360-degree leadership. Working with leaders in cultures vastly different than my own motivated me to learn what worked and what did not within those cultures. Based on the leadership of the organization I served, the current practice involved taking the model that worked in our culture and apply it to every culture. However, this was not successful. In time, I realized that each culture learned differently. The practices and educational levels varied from one country to another. Attempts to shape every educational environment to fit into the mold of one that worked in a Western setting soon presented immeasurable challenges in an Eastern and Southern setting.

Initially, I was comfortable with what worked for me and the organization. I thought the solution seemed simple enough: We could equip leaders in these countries with the necessary tools to follow the pattern previously established by the organization. It was logical and had a proven track record, but it was limited to the analytical mindset of the West. The design of the program was structured for specific settings with specific educational levels and goals. It was not a workable solution for every country and culture. We were stuck, and implementing changes would not be easy.

My effort to change the direction of the educational practices was met with resistance. I knew that to make the necessary changes I had to conduct appropriate research, provide a case study, and present information at the right time. It was a difficult time for me, and encouraging the organization to make these kinds of changes was stressful and challenging. I learned much about leadership and the Comfort Zone. Thankfully, even though I no longer work for this organization, many of the suggestions have been implemented and the organization's international influence has grown.

Life in the Comfort Zone is easy; challenging that comfort level is not. If it were, the Comfort Zone would not exist. The challenge may require learning something new, changing a current procedure or program, eliminating a position that no longer functions well, or confronting someone who holds you or the company back from growth. It could be a hundred other things. But one thought is certain: You will need courage. It takes strength of character and conviction. It also requires caution, lest you oversteer and land your organization in a worse situation. Leadership is about moving people from where they are to where they need to be, even if they don't know it. To do so, you must move out of the Comfort Zone. Challenge yourself.

Set Goals

I cannot emphasize enough the importance of setting goals in order to get out of the Comfort Zone. Goals are essential to both life and leadership. Take time to research the type of material that pushes you to learn more deeply. The relationship between vision, mission, goals and plans provides a key component to moving beyond the Comfort Zone, because the vision describes *who* you want to become in the future, inspiring action. The mission identifies *what* you will do to get there, supplying energy. The goals and plans specify exactly *how* you will achieve success, providing traction.

Take one month and do this experiment: Set a goal, or goals, for the next thirty days. Follow that up with breaking down your plan to achieve those goals into a four-week, step-by-step blueprint. Then, examine each week one day at a time. Write out what must be done each day to complete the plan for the week. After thirty days, evaluate the difference in your life before and after using goals.

Life without goals limits your potential and causes you to wander around aimlessly. By contrast, creating goals pushes you beyond the Comfort Zone to achieve greater things, because it forces you to be intentional about your actions, rather than defaulting to what is comfortable. You overcome fear, discover, practice, grow, and achieve success. This experiment will reveal just how much potential you're leaving on the table when you stumble through leadership without goals. Give it a try and you will realize how your life and leadership change in a short period of time.

Take the Risk

Just Do It! The wisdom in the Nike slogan applies to most areas of life. To get out of the Comfort Zone and move ahead, you must be willing to take some risks. Maybe it is writing that book you never thought you would write, asking for the raise you desperately need, going back to school to further your education, taking the leap into a new career, starting a family, or stepping up to lead something for your church or community. Whatever it is, now is the time to commit yourself to "Just Do It!" And let me add a slogan I heard a few years ago, "Do It Today!"

Without taking risks, most of us would not be able to walk, run, ride a bike, swim, play an instrument, participate in sports, or thousands of other tasks. Without taking risks the western hemisphere would never have been discovered. Without taking risks the United States would still be under the rule of England. Without taking risks we would all be walking or riding on a horse instead of driving a car. Without taking risks the Wright brothers would never have taken flight. Without taking risks Neil Armstrong would never have walked on the moon and space travel would only be a dream. Without taking risks the technology that connects us through the world wide web would not exist.

I've taken numerous risks in my life. Perhaps none have been greater than starting a family. The minute children are born everything changes. Taking on the responsibility of another person's life is overwhelming. Our children's existence and survival were totally dependent upon my wife and myself. Everything they would learn about life and how to cope with the world around them was based on the way we raised them. Our standards and values would provide a foundation for their own.

Whether you lead a family or an organization, success will require risks, so take them. Do the research, evaluate available resources, consult wise counsel, calculate the risks involved, and step out. Do not let fear rule your life. As many have said before, "The biggest risk is not taking it."

Before leaving this section, I want to clarify a few thoughts about risks, specifically the type of risks you face. Gordon Graham, former Sergeant with the California Highway Patrol and founder of Graham Research Consultants presented this chart to illustrate the consequences associated with the type of risk and the frequency associated with it.[15]

NDT	
High Risk	**High Risk**
Low Frequency DT	**High Frequency**
Low Risk	**Low Risk**
Low Frequency	**High Frequency**

Quadrants with high risk/high frequency, low risk/low frequency, and low risk/high frequency are not the areas of greatest concern. Whenever low risk is involved, the outcomes have less consequential value. Even though the risk is high in the high risk/high frequency quadrant, the repetitive nature suggests an ability to make better decisions because the risk is encountered more frequently.

When it comes to risk, the major area of concern falls in the high risk/low frequency quadrant. Anytime leaders face decisions characterized by high risk, considerable consequences accompany those decisions. The difficulty increases with low frequency, because it creates unexpected situations where leaders are most often unprepared, what I refer to in the next chapter as "Forced Conflict."

You will notice the high risk/low frequency quadrant is divided in half with the initials NDT (non-discretionary time) and DT (discretionary time). The greatest risk exists when you approach a high risk/low frequency situation and have little or no time (NDT) to think about the decision. However, the risk can be minimized when you have time to think about how to handle the situation and make the appropriate decision (DT). It does not eliminate high risk, or the consequences that accompany it, but with time to think, you can make decisions that minimize the consequences accompanying the risk.

Risk Management. There is more written and prescribed concerning risk management than I can possibly cover in this brief discussion. The Marine Corps follows four basic principles in application to risk management: "Risk is anticipated and managed by planning. We make risk decisions at the right level. We do not accept unnecessary risk. We accept risk when benefits outweigh costs."

According to Major Michael Castaneda, the Marines utilize the Joint Risk Assessment Matrix.[16] The matrix assesses the level of risk based on *severity* versus *probability*, i.e., *severity of hazard* and *frequency of occurrence over time*. Events that are catastrophic in nature and occur frequently over a period of time indicate an extremely high level of risk. The opposite is true of events that produce minimal or negligible impact and occur less frequently. The Risk Assessment Matrix chart provides a visual of how to determine risk levels from extremely high to low.

Risk Assessment Matrix			PROBABILITY				
			Frequency of Occurrence Over Time				
			A Frequent (Continuously experienced)	B Likely (Will occur frequently)	C Occasional (Will occur several times)	D Seldom (Unlikely; can be expected to occur)	E Unlikely (Improbable; but possible to occur)
SEVERITY — Effect of Hazard	Catastrophic (Death, Loss of Asset, Mission Capability or Unit Readiness)	I	EH	EH	H	H	M
	Critical (Severe Injury or Damage, Significantly Degraded Mission Capability or Unit Readiness)	II	EH	H	H	M	L
	Moderate (Minor Injury or Damage, Degraded Mission Capability or Unit Readiness)	III	H	M	M	L	L
	Negligible (Minimal Injury or Damage, Little or No Impact to Mission Readiness or Unit Readiness)	IV	M	L	L	L	L
			Risk Assessment Levels				
			EH=Extremely High H=High M=Medium L=Low				

The systematic and cyclical procedure used by the Marines consists of five steps: Identify Hazards, Assess Hazards, Make Risk Decisions, Implement Controls, and Supervise (and Evaluate). This process assists leaders in making informed decisions which help minimize the risk.[16]

What does this mean for you? It means you will have to make decisions that come with risk. Do not be afraid to take appropriate risks and make necessary decisions. Evaluate the level of risk using the tools provided by Graham Research Consultants or the Marine Corps. The guidelines from both will help you make appropriate decisions and minimize the negative consequences. In my exchange with Col. Dorminey, he said, "The ability and desire to take risks also grows with each risk taken. Start with small risks and as you gain comfort with evaluating alternatives and making a decision based on known conditions, you will become more adept at making decisions when the conditions are less predictable eventually arriving at a place where you can navigate even ambiguous conditions."

As a leader, you have a responsibility to evaluate where you are in your leadership and how that impacts the direction of the people you lead. The Comfort Zone is the first of four Zones, and it can be the most difficult to move beyond. At any point in your journey through the remaining Zones, you can default back to the first one. Why? Because you are more comfortable here. However, Eckhart Tolle reminds us, "Humans don't awaken in their comfort zone, they awaken when they are out of their comfort zone. This is a time of great opportunity."[17] Something must change. Although it is a time of great opportunity, once that change takes place, conflict ensues, and fear takes hold. When you begin to move outside the Comfort Zone, life introduces new challenges, which is why I turn your attention next to the battlefield—the Combat Zone.

In The Comfort Zone

1. Which characteristics of the Comfort Zone do you see in your organization's current leadership approach?

    a. Comfortable
    b. Stuck in a rut
    c. False sense of Security and Success
    d. Familiarity and Predictability
    e. Risk averse

2. On a scale of 1-5, how appropriately and effectively do your leaders communicate to the organization?

    1 ——————— 3 ——————— 5

    | Reactive | Neutral | Proactive |
    | Ineffective | | Consistent |
    | Non-existent | | Clear |

3. On a scale of 1-5, how willing and able to take risk is the leadership team within the organization?

    1 ——————— 3 ——————— 5

    | Actively | Neutral | Open to |
    | Avoids | | Change and |
    | Risk | | Risk Taking |

4. What processes and procedures are currently in place to assist the organization with change management and operational excellence? If there are none currently in place, what processes and procedures should be put in place?

5. What steps will you take to avoid returning to the Comfort Zone in the future?

Chapter Two

The Combat Zone

"No one starts a war or rather, no one in his sense ought to do so without first being clear in his mind what he intends to achieve by the war and how he intends to conduct it."
Carl von Clausewitz

Our world has been mired in conflict and unanticipated change for years. Consider the challenges introduced to the education system during the coronavirus pandemic. Education systems at every level, from elementary schools to universities, constantly wrestled with next steps in educating the youth of this nation in light of COVID-19. Administrators had to decide whether to meet in-person or online, whether to require vaccinations, whether to require masks, the appropriate distance between desks, safe social distancing, and whether to allow eating in cafeterias. Additionally, parental pressure raised the stress levels with every decision. As new variants spread across the globe, these challenges became more complicated.

Overall, parents were comfortable with the education system before the pandemic. They sent their children to school to learn and develop various social skills among their peers. And then, in March of 2020, that comfortable routine was completely disrupted—schools' sudden closures kept children at home 24/7. Parents had to help their children adjust to virtual classroom studying or take a more hands-on approach and actively teach their own children. Neither option worked well, because in many cases, both parents worked outside the home. To say parents were forced out of their Comfort Zone is a gross understatement.

This was but one of several major societal effects of the pandemic. Businesses across the nation were shut down, and many never recovered. Restaurants suffered as much, if not

more, than anyone. This single global event—one virus—
completely redefined our world. It erased practically every
comfort in our lives and moved the world into a state of chaos
and conflict. To borrow from military terminology, we could
call this new state of life the Combat Zone.

What is the Combat Zone?

As the Comfort Zone represents a place of comfort, so
the Combat Zone represents a place of combat. Here you find
conflict, challenge, difficulty, and struggle. The introduction of
change moves us out of the Comfort Zone, and with change
comes resistance. While the type of conflict familiar to the
Combat Zone may not be new to leaders, leading through
conflict presents unique circumstances that can impede the
desired progress for any organization.

Change

Tom Peters credits Kevin Kelly with saying, "It is easier
to kill an organization than it is to change it."[18] Stepping out of
the Comfort Zone involves change, whether it is forced or
initiated, and change strikes at our core. Why is change so
difficult? Perhaps, as I once heard, "The need for change does
not outweigh the pain of change." Another reason is because
people tend to anticipate the worst. Most organizations resist
change because they assume that change can *only* bring about
chaos. But it does not have to be this way; indeed, some
organizations thrive on continual change, even the chaos that
accompanies it. They embody Tony Richard's advice that
change be "intentional for positive transformation."[19] While not
all change results in positive transformation, intentional
leadership can move organizations in a positive direction amidst
change.

For many organizations, recent history has reshaped concepts that involve change. In current organizational climate, businesses find themselves *living* change rather than implementing it. The constant nature of change has created what is known as VUCA (Volatility, Uncertainty, Complexity, and Ambiguity). In an article discussing the subject, Mark Marone, director of research and thought leadership for Dale Carnegie and Associates, defines each term: "Volatility refers to the volume and speed at which change happens. Uncertainty is the difficulty in making accurate predictions for the future. Complexity refers to the number of factors in play and the way each factor influences others, and ambiguity, a lack of clarity on how to interpret the available information."[20] He went on to claim that VUCA has produced a need for roles in change management (a systematic approach to *how*) and change leadership (a focus on attitudes, skills, capabilities driving *why*).

Regardless of how we feel about change, it is an inevitable part of life. How you respond to change is what makes the difference. While there are many possible reactions to change, a few common threads seem to emerge.

Fear. People experience fear for a variety of reasons. The list of phobias is mind-boggling. Included in the list is *change*. Why do people fear change? One reason is because change is difficult, and people lack a clear understanding of why the change is being made. As one author put it,

> Sometimes, the **way** leaders introduce change only creates **more** resistance.

"Knowledge gaps are filled with fear instead of faith."[21] Leaders often make changes with limited, ineffective, or even nonexistent communication. In these cases, they fail to illuminate how they came to the decision to make the change, why this change is being made, when the change will be implemented, how it will be implemented, who will be

47

involved, and why the present moment is the right time for the change. When these gaps in knowledge exist, people experience fear. Resistance soon follows. Sometimes, the *way* leaders introduce change only creates *more* resistance.

Another reason people fear change is because they often perceive change as propelling them in a negative direction, which tends to push people into a self-preservation mode. Major Castaneda told me, "When conditions want to be overridden by self-preservation, it is associated with fear, and fear uncontrolled is a dangerous, dangerous thing. It can cause you to injure yourself or others recklessly. It can lead you to, under certain conditions, make right decisions and preserve life, or do more damage. What a leader does under these conditions really defines who they are as a leader."

People are uncertain about the effects of change and the fear generated by change becomes so strong that any attempt at further change is strongly resisted. Fear is not unique to anyone, but the responses created by fear can be quite diverse. At times, fear is healthy and provides an element of protection. At other times, fear only makes you reckless and holds you back. While it is natural to experience fear to some degree when facing change, the decisions you make in relationship to your fear determine the outcome.

Most of the time, fear strikes when we take that first step out of the Comfort Zone. This is not the only time fear creeps into leadership, but it tends to be the point of origin. Fear is a reality that prevents leaders from doing things they would normally do, but it also causes them to do things they would *not* do under normal circumstances. Change, and the fear it creates, can be destructive to leadership and can set any organization on the wrong course. It can potentially shackle your ability to overcome and move toward greater self-discovery, positive growth and development, along with real success. When fear exists, organizations lack the psychological safety essential to creative innovation and team morale. If the environment is psychologically unsafe, people remain in their comfort zone.

Anger. Anger is another common response to change, especially if the person is against the proposed change. Politics ranks as one of the most divisive subjects in the world today, and religion follows at a close second. When the two are intertwined in a discussion, the atmosphere can be explosively volatile. A scroll through posts on social media will easily illustrate my point. Regardless of which side people stand on politically, when the opposing side is elected or directing changes in the judicial system, anger rears its ugly head. The vile expressions of anger that are often presented from behind the safety of a keyboard and computer screen are enough to make most people nauseous. It is disheartening to witness the way people take to social media platforms to spew their hatred toward anyone who does not agree with them politically. Tragically, the same vitriol also rears its head in conversations about religion.

> *It is disheartening to witness the way people take to social media platforms to spew their hatred toward anyone who does not agree with them politically.*

People do not like change. I get it. I am not always a fan of change either, especially if it is change for the sake of change. The older I get, the less I like change. Yet, it is unavoidable. For example, as we age, we experience all kinds of changes in our bodies. For me, the creaks I have begun to hear in my joints sound more like tires creeping down a gravel road. I remember my dad saying, "Son, this getting old ain't all it's cracked up to be." Boy was he right! Another one of his favorite sayings was, "You have to be tough to get old." Also, a true statement.

Some things are only understood by experience, and the changes that occur with age is one of them. This is but one example of the change that happens all around you, whether you agree with it or not. Getting angry does not help resolve your dislike for change.

Denial. People often respond to change with denial, especially after they've moved through fear and anger. Denial can be one of the most difficult stages in the process. According to the Kübler-Ross Grief Cycle, a few of the symptoms that characterize denial in processing grief are avoidance, confusion, elation, shock, and fear.[22] As applied to change within an organization or a family, denial may look like refusal to admit there is a need for change or refusal to accept the facts surrounding the proposed change. It can also take the form of an exaggerated retreat or becoming reclusive.

Denial exists when organizations avoid change and operate with a methodology from a previous era. Oddly, these organizations expect that by holding onto these practices, they will grow as they did years ago. Remember that without change, growth cannot occur. This is true even down to the biological level—and it is true in the metaphorical sense, as well. No one experiences growth and remains the same as they were before. Living in denial of these facts, attempting to run away from them, only causes greater challenges.

Denial generates a strong desire to retreat and become more reclusive. In denial, we withdraw from everyone and everything. In some ways, it's as though we believe we can hide from the change and not be affected. For example, many people in the world have become increasingly antisocial in response to changes caused by the coronavirus pandemic. Many people were relentless in their calls to return to the way things were pre-pandemic. While appealing, the reality of this plan seems highly unlikely. If you do not find a way to overcome denial, walking down this reclusive path can result in a socially introverted mindset.

Obviously, denial affects people differently. Of course, denial does not eliminate change or prevent it from occurring. Denial is just a glorified form of delay. In reality, it is only delaying acceptance in someone's mind. When denial is allowed to rule your life, you miss out on the experience of change, and you unconsciously and openly hinder growth and progress initiated by change.

Embrace. When leaders introduce change, embracing the change is the desired result. With this comes a host of positive traits and characteristics that promote growth and development. Once you reach the ability to embrace change, doors of opportunity open in abundant ways. As a leader in the Space Force, Col. Dorminey told me that when people embrace change, "they are bought in and will work hard to see the change to fruition. Someone who simply accepts the change, when met with the first obstacle they will often stop and wait for someone else to make a move to either fix or abandon the change." Opportunities to learn, expand, reprioritize, and build on a stronger foundation for the future occur when you embrace change. Doing so ushers in a time of transformation. Your mind is transformed as you anticipate new experiences, develop more intimate relationships with others, strengthen your talents and abilities, and press forward to greater achievement.

I will be the first to admit that not all change is good. As you likely understand by now, change should not be introduced for its own sake or without careful consideration. But when you invest in positive change, your confidence grows. The ability to adapt to change will also encourage others to witness the positive benefits that come with the acceptance of change, and it might shorten the life cycle of reactions to change in the future.

Fear, anger, and denial become contagious when left unchecked. Introducing change creates emotions that often spread throughout an organization leaving a wake of discouragement and destruction in its path. Leaders can address each response with one word: communication. Healthy communication reduces fear because people fear what they do not know. Clearly communicate the details behind why decisions were

> *No one ever complained about having too much information in the midst of change, but they certainly grumble about being left in the dark.*

made, how you plan to implement and move through the change, and what you will do if something does not work out as planned. No one ever complained about having too much information in the midst of change, but they certainly grumble about being left in the dark. Similarly, communication can prevent anger by helping people feel empowered. It can also reduce the frequency and severity of most heated moments. When people get angry, you need to know why they are angry and how to address the source of their anger. Communication is critical.

The same is true when faced with denial. As with fear and anger, denial is a cry for healthy communication. Learning how to communicate openly prior to, during, and after change helps reduce the desire for this mindset. People may still struggle with wanting to run away from the change, but when you effectively present these changes and provide a safe space for discussing them, a calmer and more peaceful atmosphere emerges. People are less likely to live in denial or seek retreat when confronted with the facts and guided through the upheaval. People want to know they are heard and that someone cares enough to listen. They also want leaders who explain the details of change, the decision to make the change, and what the future looks like because of the change. Communication directs everyone toward greater acceptance and support.

Resistance

Resistance is the cornerstone characteristic of the Combat Zone. Any time change is introduced, there will be a level of resistance. Sometimes, you will experience resistance from those who desire nothing more than to stop the changes introduced. In such moments, you might feel this strong opposition comes from those who are against you, which is a possibility. However, resistance can be good for development. As William Wrigley Jr. once said, "When two men in a business always agree, one of them is unnecessary."[23] The idea here is that some level of push-back ensures that the best ideas emerge. Without this resistance, ideas are left unchecked and can ultimately result in failure. Not all resistance is a bad thing— sometimes, it's just what you need.

However, resistance can take on a nasty and negative presence, especially if the intent is to resist *any* change, regardless of its wisdom. Every organization has people who never want change and resist it with every fiber of their being. They will go to any length to stop progress. Even though change introduces greater potential for growth and development, these enemies of change feel compelled to stop it, and they are convinced it is the right thing to do. Step back, evaluate the resistance, and consider the right perspective. Sadly, the resistance encountered when change is introduced usually leads to some form or level of conflict.

Conflict

In the Combat Zone, conflict is the norm. Conflict pops up in every area of life. Conflict arises in the home between husbands and wives, parents and children, and among siblings. You find conflict in the workplace between employers and employees, as well as among coworkers. Conflict arises between neighbors over boundary lines, care of property, and noise levels. Conflict occurs between teachers, in children's athletic programs, students who experience bullying, and there is even conflict between rival schools. Our politics are imbued with conflict, and the long-term effects of the associated division and destruction are immeasurable. Dare I even mention the conflict on social media platforms? Social media has become the new arena for conflict. What appears to many as an opportunity to express their thoughts behind the safety of a keyboard and screen has resulted in new levels of conflict and cyberbullying that the world is only beginning to fully understand.

What's more, conflict not only exists in situations of opposition with others, but it can also exist within an individual. Internal conflict is described as the battle that occurs when we struggle with what we may desire versus what we know is right or best. This type of conflict occurs when what I value (losing weight, good health, longer life) is in conflict with what I desire in the moment (sleeping in instead of exercising, eating an extra piece of pie, or excessive indulgences, such as alcohol or drugs).

Several leaders I've talked to indicate that culturally we have lost the ability to manage conflict. Everyone agrees that conflict will happen in every area of life, but it seems that many have lost the tools needed to discuss and work through the issues faced in their home, community, workplace, political, or religious setting. To further complicate the discussion, most schools and workplaces share space with four or five generations of people. Tim Elmore's team suggests the need for a strong generational quotient (GQ).[24] Leaders understand the benefits of IQ and EQ in the workplace. However, GQ spans the generational gap. When attempting to cross the generational divide challenges often lead to greater conflict. Instead of collaborating, people clash. Misunderstanding quickly moves to frustration, which results in an impasse. Rather than stereotyping each generation, or allowing frustration to hinder a healthy working environment, a two-way street where understanding flows both ways is desperately needed.

The tools in this book are designed to guide you through conflict on all levels, in every arena, and between each generation. Regardless of the context in which the conflict arises, it likely falls into one of two categories: forced conflict or initiated conflict. Both present unique challenges, and how you lead through them is different.

Forced conflict. Forced conflict is exactly what you might think: It is conflict that exists when change is forced on people. Forced conflict is characterized by the unexpected and, as a result, no one is prepared for it. When conflict is forced onto an individual or an organization, people are often caught off guard, and they may respond with knee-jerk reactions.

The most obvious example of forced conflict is the COVID-19 pandemic. No one expected what happened. No one could have predicted it or the outcome. In the beginning, discussions centered around short-term changes, and most people assumed it would only last a few weeks or maybe a month. As time moved on, it became more and more apparent this global pandemic would reshape our daily life. The world continues to struggle with the effects of the coronavirus and the multiplicity of variants that exist, even years after the onset of the pandemic.

The pandemic is not the only example that highlights the adversity forced conflict brings. Forced conflict created by life circumstances, such as natural disasters, have been witnessed in tornadoes across the United States, which have destroyed property and taken lives of those in their paths. Hurricanes (Andrew, Katrina, and Harvey) and tsunamis (Tōhoku, Indian Ocean, and Sulawesi), along with the flooding associated with these disasters, left a wake of destruction that forced conflict on those affected by them. Volcanic eruptions, such as Vesuvius (79 AD), Tambora (1815), Mount St. Helen's (1980), Nevado del Ruiz (1985), and Kelud (1990), also represent events that forced conflict on countries throughout the world. The devastation changed the direction of life for all impacted by them.

Another illustration of forced conflict surfaces with the challenges of illness, disease, and tragic accidents. These circumstances can cause our lives to spin completely out of control. When someone faces a terminal disease, life-or-death decisions must be made. No one expects these times of turmoil, and most are unprepared when they occur. The result is forced conflict. I've known several friends and colleagues around the world whose lives were cut short by a traffic accident. Their families suffer from forced conflict. These events are never expected, and we are left to ask, "How is it possible to prepare for them?"

> When leaders face situations of forced conflict, their leadership is more critical than ever.

When leaders face situations of forced conflict, their leadership is more critical than ever. You must act quickly. However, let me share a few suggestions to address the nature of circumstances associated with forced conflict. First, establish procedures in advance to deal with potential sources of forced conflict. Inevitably, leaders will face situations out of their control. I've heard all my life that to be forewarned is to be forearmed. According to Col. Dorminey, aviators have what is called "BOLD FACE checklists which are for emergencies and often memorized for quick reaction to inflight emergencies. In many cases they are derived from accident investigations or debriefs. The lessons of a previous mishap are used to create the BOLDFACE to prevent a mishap in the future." The idea suggests that we need to take as many precautionary measures as possible to prepare. I realize we cannot fully prepare for every possible scenario but consider a few advance steps: (1) Ask a few "what if" questions. What if x or y happens; (2) Make a list of essential contacts; (3) Connect to others who would be affected by the event; (4) Set aside potential financial resources and other essential needs; (5) Never lose hope—think positively.

Second, gather as much intel as possible. Your decisions hinge on a comprehensive understanding of the gravity involved. When the world became aware of the pandemic, information about the spread of the virus and protective measures was premium. The speed at which decisions are made with the information gathered determines the outcome for every person you lead. Therefore, it is a top priority to make decisions with the highest level of information available. However, the key word here is "available." Every leader must be careful to avoid being paralyzed waiting on additional information which may or may not come or arrive in time to make a decision.

Third, be willing to adjust as needed. Once decisions are made, situations may change. I remember explicit details provided during practice from my high school basketball coach. He showed us how to move the basketball from one side of the court to the other. The plan was to get someone open for a clear and easy basket. As the ball was passed from one side to the other, he explained how the defense would react and move in a certain way, which would allow the ball to go inside to our post player for a close shot. However, the defenses we played against did not get the information coach provided, because they almost never moved as he said they would. Therefore, we had to be willing and able to adjust. Leading an organization is the same. When facing a situation of forced conflict, decisions are made based on the best information available, but once movement starts, the situation may turn in an unexpected direction. When that happens, you must be willing to adjust.

Fourth, communicate incessantly. Nothing is more important than communicating every step of the way. Communicate the prearranged procedures for conflict. Communicate the intel you've gathered and how it affects the decisions being made. Communicate adjustments made to address changes as they occur. Communication is the key to dealing with every level of forced conflict. The more you communicate, the more support you will have from those who assist you in working through the conflict.

At some point or another, forced conflict befalls everyone. The changes that occur with forced conflict can drive you down a path of confusion and concern. As a leader, you can take steps to address the challenges that accompany forced conflict, but you cannot avoid it entirely. However, not all conflict is forced. Leaders can avoid or minimize the resistance that accompanies conflict when change happens if they learn how to initiate changes in an appropriate way.

Initiated Conflict. Initiated conflict looks completely different than forced conflict. While the conflict is still present, it is not the result of being caught off-guard and unprepared. When people are prepared for, or at least aware of upcoming change, there is a level of expectation. They may dislike the forthcoming changes, but they have the opportunity to mentally prepare. Therefore, when change is introduced, conflict is minimized because of the preparation and expectation associated with upcoming changes.

Initiated conflict begins with planning. Remember that the manner in which change is initiated can make or break a smooth transition. Your plans must identify at least five key components: when the change will occur, who the change will affect, how the change will improve current circumstances, what the change requires, and why.

Planning must be accompanied by developing good negotiation skills. Chris Voss states, "Negotiation is the heart of collaboration. It is what makes conflict meaningful and productive for all parties."[25] Learning these skills will strengthen your approach to initiating any change, thus minimizing the resistance.

It is critical to explain why this change is being made and why now. Do not be afraid to share the details of discussions surrounding the development of the change. It is essential to identify everyone's individual roles and expectations for the change so they can further prepare. Inform them of steps needed to implement the change. As a leader, you also need to define your own role, which *must* include action and communication throughout the process. It is critical for leaders to communicate amidst change. This communication involves more than just telling everyone a change is coming. If you want buy-in from your followers, two-way communication in the information gathering and planning phase is essential. Once you enlist the "boots on the ground" in strategic planning, you can then communicate the process leading to change.

If possible, meet with followers one-on-one and allow them to ask questions, share ideas, and explore how they can help make this transition successful. If your organization is too large for one-on-one meetings, set aside designated events at which people can express their grievances and ask questions. Memos, bulletin board posts, emails, texts, or public announcements leave people confused at best and flat-out combative at worst. The most effective way to get the majority involved is sitting down and talking with those affected face-to-face.

Leaders who proactively plan and initiate change with open and transparent communication will find that people are much less resistant. With less resistance, leaders can devote their energy to implementing the change, rather than mediating conflict among followers. The result provides a win-win scenario for the entire team.

It is important to note that initiated conflict and forced conflict can sometimes be two sides of the same coin. You must be aware of perspective during times of conflict. It is highly probable that each side of the conflict sees from a completely different perspective. On one side, you may believe you are initiating the conflict, while the other side believes you are forcing the conflict. Your decisions at the executive level affect everyone in the organization. Those decisions can require hard conversations impacting the employment or involvement of staff, faculty, employees, and volunteers. You are tasked with leading through these turbulent times with an understanding of both sides while minimizing resistance, valuing everyone involved, and maximizing the overall emotional health and physical wellbeing of the people who work for the organization. Let me say up front, few tasks of a leader are more difficult than this.

> *When communication is not prevalent, the atmosphere can deteriorate quickly and lead to far worse outcomes.*

Effectively leading through change or conflict requires communication. When communication is not prevalent, the atmosphere can deteriorate quickly and lead to far worse outcomes, such as the devastation and destruction of war. I realize there are times you must confront difficult situations and address difficult conversations, but as Edwin Starr sings in "War,"

War has shattered many a young man's dreams.
Made him disabled, bitter, and mean.
Life is much too short and precious to spend fighting
wars these days.
War can't give life; it can only take it away.[26]

The bottom line is that you will find yourself in the
Combat Zone at one point or another, and how you approach
combat makes all the difference. You must learn how to lead
through it. However, there is more to the Combat Zone than
change, resistance, and conflict.

Insecurity

Insecurity debilitates the greatest of leaders. Even when
you know you are right about a specific direction or qualified to
discuss a certain topic, the negative criticism from opposition
can create a level of insecurity that destroys your confidence
and influence. This situation can result from conflict with those
who oppose you, with personal internal conflicts, or both.
Regardless, the tension forces you to question yourself and your
ability to lead.

What causes a leader to experience these feelings of
insecurity or to lack self-confidence? Often, the answer relates
to the unique traits of the individual. But some common causes
emerge. According to Melanie Greenberg, there are four main
causes of insecurity.[27]

Recent failures or rejections. When a student
diligently prepares for a major exam and then fails, their
confidence approaching the next exam is weakened. When
someone spends countless hours preparing material to pitch a
new product, sales approach, or safety guideline to owners of a
company, only to have it rejected, self-confidence can be

damaged. Any sort of rejection or failure can impact the way you think about your leadership. Failure and rejection make it difficult to think with confidence about leading others. Greenberg says, "The biggest negative contributor to unhappiness is the ending of a relationship, followed by the death of a spouse, job loss, and negative health events. Since unhappiness also influences your self-esteem, failure and rejection can deliver a double whammy to your confidence."

Social anxiety. The anxiety that social media causes is immeasurable, especially among young people, but they are not alone. Movies like *The Social Dilemma*[28] have increased awareness about the dangers of social media platforms. A quick look at the impact of social media in the presidential election of 2020 is proof enough to illustrate the anxiety created and the division developed among families, religious circles, work, and even friendships. Anyone can fall prey to these dangers.

Anxiety raises its ugly head when you constantly seek approval from your social circle, either online or in person, only to be met with disapproval. When acceptance and approval are the goals, any form of disapproval creates insecurity and lower levels of self-confidence. While young people deal with the daily pressures of social acceptance, the odds of suffering from anxiety increase as their sense of security and confidence are based on a preconceived approval rating. Greenberg contributes to this discussion by saying, "Many of us experience a lack of confidence in social situations like parties, family gatherings, interviews, and dates. The fear of being evaluated by others—and found to be lacking—can lead you to feel anxious and self-conscious."

Perfectionism. The third cause strikes close to home for many, especially me. Different levels of perfectionism exist from one individual to the next. The idea of "paralysis by analysis" seems to characterize the concept. When you feel as though you can never make a decision, get it right, or complete a task because you always need to research one more article or book or interview, these feelings can hinder your growth and development. For some leaders, perfectionism destroys the opportunity to help others reach their potential, because the performance is never as good as the leader thinks it could be if they did it themselves. They micromanage to the point of frustration, which leads to giving up. Greenberg goes on to say, "If you are constantly disappointed and blaming yourself for being anything less than perfect, you will start to feel insecure and unworthy. While trying your best and working hard can give you an advantage, other aspects of perfectionism are unhealthy." In addition to these three leading causes, Greenberg alludes to a fourth cause of insecurity that is noteworthy.

Past experiences. The way you were raised, the influences in your life when you were young, your educational background, and even the smallest of comments made during those formative years of life play a major role in developing your security or insecurity. For example, children who are abused emotionally, physically, or sexually often develop deep insecurities as a consequence. Greenberg points out, "Past experience can feed your sense of not belonging, not feeling important or interesting, or just not being good enough." Let me share a story that illustrates the point about past experiences.

Consider an employee who gets the opportunity of a lifetime to lead a group of people he has known for ten years. Let's call him Sam. This is a special group, and he is excited to work with them. At first, everything is paradise—almost too good to be true. He learns quickly why the first few years on the job are referred to as the honeymoon phase. Sam gains a great deal of popularity with *nearly* everyone on the job. Routine sets in, along with the daily grind of work. Before long, colleagues become a bit jealous and start picking apart Sam's presentations. Nothing is good enough, and everything Sam tries to do is always wrong. Immediately, Sam recalls the verbal and mental abuse of his father. Nothing he did growing up was ever good enough. He remembered the constant barrage of insults, including that he would "never amount to anything," and that he was "good for nothing." Soon, he is no longer performing at the same level. His confidence is shaken. He quickly becomes insecure in his job performance and in his ability to work with others. While most co-workers loved the work Sam did, the few who were vocal began to wear him down. He became discouraged, frustrated, and doubtful of his own ability to perform well. The effects of his childhood left a lasting impression on Sam and reflecting on the comments from coworkers left him struggling with self-confidence. This is the type of insecurity created from past experiences.

Everyone experiences failure or rejection at some point in life. The world lives in the realm of social media interaction. The concept of perfectionism takes many forms at home and on the job. These three components, along with past experiences, all factor into our security and confidence levels. Regardless of its cause, insecurity can be crippling if not properly addressed.

Casualties

Whenever conflict arises in the Combat Zone, there will be casualties. From a military perspective, I am aware of the casualties associated with combat. My description of casualties is not intended to equate to the tragic loss of life in these situations. While the proverbial casualties of the Combat Zone could never compare to casualties of war, all conflict has externalities.

When conflict exists within our homes and organizations, there are often casualties. For example, children become casualties of contentious divorces. One parent may manipulate their ex-spouse before, during, and after a divorce. Children hear the anger spewed about their father or mother. They grow up in two homes with one parent in each, and often with a stepparent. Neither parent wants to discipline the child for fear the child will not want to be with them, or worse they use the child against their former spouse. Over and over, children get caught in the crossfire of their parents' Combat Zone. Rarely do parents understand the impact on the child's life until it is too late.

Similar circumstances unfold in organizations. You may have worked for a hot-and-cold boss at some point: Each day you wait with anxious anticipation to see which attitude you are going to get. If they are in a good mood, everything moves along smoothly. However, if they are not, everyone walks on eggshells hoping not to upset them. Employees live in constant fear for their jobs. One mistake sets off fireworks, and heads usually roll. Employees become casualties. Whenever possible, they look for a different department or a new employer entirely.

At times, entire businesses become the casualties of conflict. As I have discussed, the conflict introduced by the coronavirus pandemic flipped the world upside down. News reports constantly highlighted the challenges employers face with hiring enough people to operate. "Now Hiring" signs were posted in most businesses. On one instance, I remember pulling up to a drive-thru window because the inside of the store was closed. When I approached the window, I discovered why. There were only three employees. Two were cooks, and the other person had to take care of the window. Situations like these were not unique. Many businesses across the country became casualties to the economic downturn that confronted them, and it left them feeling anxious, and many closed permanently.

Acceptance and Consensus

One of the most difficult things to overcome in leadership is trying to please everyone. You may want to make everyone happy because you are concerned someone will say something bad about you, have nothing to do with you, or worse, leave your organization. The tendency is becoming more common, and it is consuming. When people leave, it places you in a position where you often lack the type of committed and quality people needed for success. Attempting to prevent it can become a problem, especially when those attempts cloud your better judgment or eat up all your time.

I understand the need to fit in, to have acceptance, and to enjoy a sense of belonging. During my first year of college, the "in thing" to do was to join a social club. Private colleges referred to them as social clubs instead of fraternities since there were no connections to a national chapter. I learned quickly there were clubs I wanted to join and some I needed to avoid. A few of the clubs were designated for athletes, and some for certain levels of education, or as they were referred to, "the nerdy clubs." I finally settled on a club that forty years ago seemed to be the right fit—the Knights. Something sounded right about that designation, and I was excited.

The process of joining the Knights involved a litany of steps, the first of which required an invitation from a current member of the club. Once invited, the next step required candidates to engage in a weeklong series of ritualistic practices that included embarrassing, silly, strange, and unpredictable acts at the whim of current members. The third step was the most brutal, as each potential inductee spent about three hours pushed, pulled, tripped, and guided from one station to another eating strange things (I have no idea what we ate!), participating in frightening activities, experiencing the painful feeling of unknown objects/creatures poured into our pants legs as we lay flat on our backs with legs held high in the air, and riding around to some strange destinations (I still have no clue where they took us!) all while blindfolded. I am sure the ones conducting these ceremonial rituals had a blast. As future members, it was anything but fun. It is amazing to think about what we will do to fit in, be accepted, or belong. It all seemed worth it to take that final step—being dubbed a Knight. That was the moment I felt most accepted throughout the whole year.

Not everyone became a Knight. Not everyone was accepted. Not everyone completed the criteria established by the club, but for those who did, few moments compare. Although I was elated over the challenges set before me to become a Knight, going to such great lengths for acceptance was dangerous. The same goes for leaders who are willing to go to extremes to be accepted or improve their approval rating. In many of these extreme cases, leaders think that once they have the approval rating they need, they will have more support and influence in the future but this just isn't the case. Once decisions are made that are met with resistance the feeling of acceptance diminishes and the vicious cycle of trying to fit in continues.

You need to know that if every decision requires one hundred percent approval, the minority will always rule—and they know it.

When I say I understand the need to fit in, to have acceptance, and to enjoy a sense of belonging, I have a rich history to support the claim. However, I also know the dangers that arise for leaders when they are so affected by the opinions of others and the desire for acceptance that they cannot make a decision without approval from everyone.

You need to know that if every decision requires one hundred percent approval, the minority will always rule—and they know it. Everything moves along well until a decision is made that goes against one person, usually someone with certain skills or money. They don't like it, they disagree with it, and they voice their opinion more loudly than anyone else. As a leader, you fear that if you go through with the decision, this person will leave and take their skills and/or money with them. The result? You appease this one person and move forward to something else. Wow! When written in black and white, it seems like a ludicrous thought; but in real life, it happens all the time. It is killing us. You become stagnant. You live in the Comfort Zone, because the moment you step out of it, someone disagrees, conflict ensues, fear raises its ugly head, and you go right back to where everything was comfortable.

This type of pandering to avoid conflict must change. Leaders who have the courage to take a stand, make informed decisions, and take appropriate action, even at the risk of a few people disagreeing with the direction, are desperately needed. If you are unwilling to do so, then why are *you* leading? Let the people who control your decisions have the reins. This kind of manipulation has been the rule far more than the exception.

I am convinced that leaders have a responsibility to listen to everyone they lead. How else do they learn the strengths and weaknesses, needs, concerns, ideas, and desires of those entrusted to their leadership? But the concept of making decisions *only* on the basis of total consensus is destructive. Not only is it ineffective—leaving people feeling insecure and lacking confidence—but it also creates frustration and hinders you from leading effectively. When this approach is engrained in the culture of your organization, the result produces a generation of people who want nothing to do with leading. Without leaders, a gap is left leaving people extremely confused, lost, and wandering around aimlessly. As I was once told, the antidote for this is "an absolute focus on the mission. All decisions should be made to advance the mission and vision. Everything else is secondary and either supportive or a distraction."

Uncertainty and the Unknown

Uncertainty and the unknown are distinct but related characteristics of the Combat Zone. Uncertainty is often caused by the unknown. While we tend to think of uncertainty as a strictly negative concept, Carl von Clausewitz's explained another interpretation: "Although our intellect always longs for clarity and certainty, our nature often finds uncertainty fascinating."[29] Clausewitz viewed uncertainty with a positive flare, one which left doors of opportunity open for growth and success. While some see the idea of uncertainty as a challenge that excites them to push ahead, others are terrified by the risk associated with uncertainty about the future.

The world is constantly mired in uncertainty. One need not look beyond the headlines of the New York Times on any given day to see endless examples of uncertainty in our world. It may be a pandemic, Russia's invasion of Ukraine, historical flooding, or mass shootings. In 2008, it was an economic crisis and in 2001, it was the war on terrorism. Similar examples are scattered throughout history. Consider the uncertainty associated with World War I, the Great Depression, and World War II that followed. Prior to these events, there were challenges of uncertainty connected to the Civil War, one of the bloodiest and most divisive events in our history.

Uncertainty begs the questions: What have we learned from these experiences? Will everyone be satisfied to return to everything as it was before the conflict? How will the conflict find resolution? Will other organizations or world leaders get involved and to what level? How will we take advantage of the opportunities presented during these crises to grow future leaders? Uncertainty is the shroud that surrounds our world leaders, and fear looms. If you only knew what the future holds, would you really want to know?

Determining how to lead through the uncertainty of a crisis is overwhelming, and it can cause short-sighted leadership. Rather than setting three-to-five-year goals, organizations make their plans on a week-by-week basis. Many organizations wonder if they will still be open five years from now. For some, there is concern about whether they will be open next year,

> *You can eliminate most of your fears about uncertainty and the unknown with this simple step: Prepare tomorrow's leaders today.*

or even next week. In their short-sightedness, they often neglect to train tomorrow's leaders.

No one can ever know the future with certainty. But the one thing you can know about the future is this: If you prepare leaders now, the future is far more secure than if you wait until the future to begin preparation. You can eliminate most of your fears about uncertainty and the unknown with this simple step: Prepare tomorrow's leaders today.

A Lack of Trust

Entire books have been written about trust as it relates to leadership. Trust is the most valuable and treasured commodity of any leader. The Franklin Covey organization built its core values based on Stephen Covey's book *The Speed of Trust*.[30] Trust, according to Covey, is connected to five principles: credibility, behavior, alignment, reputation, and contribution. He also explains that not extending trust can be the greatest risk of all.

When you lead in the Combat Zone, your first concern involves trust. Who can you trust to help you, support you, walk alongside you, and back you up when making decisions? But along with knowing who *you* can trust, others need to know they can trust you and your leadership. What creates a lack of trust in leadership? What must be done to establish trust when facing situations identified by characteristics in the Combat Zone?

There are numerous reasons for a lack of trust in leadership. For example, when leaders are lazy, make poor decisions, fail to communicate effectively, drive a self-seeking agenda, lack courage, or do not trust their teams, a lack of trust flourishes. Best-selling author and consultant, Shelley Smith, claims, "A lack of trust in the workplace is the virus that can create a diseased workplace culture. It often begins with leadership and spreads throughout the team, leading to a cycle of unhealthy responses that affect engagement and productivity."[31] The result is a dysfunctional and combative environment that leads to greater conflict.

An example of Smith's point occurred in 2001 when Enron, an innovative energy company, declared the largest bankruptcy in U.S. history. In a twentieth anniversary article for Time Magazine, Simon Constable indicated that Americans lost trust in the stock market because of Enron's failings. However, the lack of trust went deeper than just market investments. According to Constable, "While lack of trust in the market is a direct consequence of Enron's mega fraud, the indirect consequences of government actions also seem to have hurt Main Street USA."[32] He indicated that Enron's fraudulent lack of transparency sent ripples throughout the stock market. Legislators passed the Sarbanes-Oxley bill in 2002 that made it more challenging for companies to become an IPO (Initial Public Offering). As Constable put it, "The Sarbanes-Oxley regulations have chased away some investing opportunities from the public market to the private ones." The design of these regulations was to implement greater transparency within organizations and minimize the lack of trust Enron created. However, the bureaucracy tied to filling out new forms, ambiguity in the law, and the lack of clarity for non-compliance resulted in fewer risks on the part of entrepreneurs.

Even though Enron's executives were convicted and went to prison, the impact of the scandal left a black mark in the minds of investors. Companies were more likely to remain private until they became much larger. When organizations fail to be transparent, the lack of trust between stakeholders and leaders causes a wave of dysfunction that has only been rivaled in the political arena.

Few areas have experienced trust issues more than politics. One such event that became a national turning point in matters of trust was the Watergate Scandal in the 1970s. Richard Nixon resigned on August 4, 1974, after serving six years as the President of the United States. Many believe his resignation was an attempt to escape impeachment after efforts to burglarize the Democratic National Committee headquarters in the Watergate complex were discovered. According to Michael Hardy, the impact of the Watergate era opened the eyes of the American public to the depth of political scandal, which raised concerns related to trust in the country's leadership.[33] While this was not the first, nor the last, of scandals rocking America's political scene, the result of each is the same. These events create a lack of trust in the American government by its people.

The world of religion has also experienced scandalous circumstances leaving many congregants with a lack of trust in their leaders. Names like Jim Bakker, Jimmy Swaggart, Ted Haggard, Bill Hybels, Tony Alamo, and Mark Driscoll are associated with various sex scandals over the last forty years that impacted the faith of those entrusted to their leadership. My intent is not to indict one person or religious organization above another. No religious group is immune to the struggles that often come with leaders in the public eye.

Let me also note that the scrutiny of religious leaders is not limited to the accusations of immorality against these

> *Whether business, politics, or religion, the world is a different place when faith and trust show up.*

figures. Accusations of fraud, stealing, and corruption are a few additional issues plaguing the world of religion. When it comes to matters of faith and religious leaders, many desire a stronger relationship with God, but they lack trust in those who claim to know the way.

A close friend of trust is faith. Whether business, politics, or religion, the world is a different place when faith and trust show up. Fear seems to melt away and courage stands in its place. At some point in life, you will face situations where you must consider, "Do I really believe in the vision and direction of the organization?" "Do I trust my team?" "Does my team trust my leadership?" And most importantly, "Will I allow my lack of faith or trust to hinder me from who and what I need to be in this moment?" I've learned it is a lot easier to cling to what you believe when living within the comforts of your own home, in the security of your subdivision. I realize no location is completely safe, but mentally, it feels more unsafe when one is physically far away from that place of comfort and familiarity. It is difficult to feel safe and secure when you are in a strange city where the language is unknown, where there is no internet access or phone service, and you do not know who to ask for help. This is exactly how it feels when trust is lost, you lose faith in yourself, and those who follow lose trust in you.

When approaching leadership, you can be paralyzed by insecurity when faced with uncertainty and confronted by the unknown. The challenges of acceptance and consensus open the door to making excuses. Ultimately, there is a lack of trust, which is usually the underlying cause for the other issues. But you do not have to remain in this place. You have the choice of taking steps to help you advance into greater success.

How Can You Lead Through the Combat Zone?

As Zig Ziglar expressed, "Fear has two meanings: 'Forget Everything And Run' or 'Face Everything And Rise.' The choice is yours."[34] Fear, which is usually the first symptom that accompanies conflict, is not always a bad thing. You must conquer it and not let it conquer you. According to Dale Carnegie, "If you want to conquer fear, don't sit home and think about it. Go out and get busy."[35] Fear does not resolve itself when you sit around thinking about it. You must act. Here are six suggestions to help you move away from the fear raised by conflict and lead toward a better Zone.

Preparation

Life changes in direct proportion to your preparation. Every military leader I interviewed explicitly identified the necessity of preparation. I have taught public speaking for several years. Without exception, the less prepared students were, the greater their fear when standing before others. Preparation is critical to minimize fear. The idea closely ties to the words of Vice Admiral Bucchi, "Know yourself, know your people, and know the threat." When you are secure with these three thoughts, you are better prepared to lead through fear caused by conflict.

You will almost always experience some level of nervousness, but when fear grips you, it can shut you down. The reason is usually a lack of preparation. I realize you cannot be prepared for every event and situation in life. Life brings unexpected moments that catch you off guard—forced conflicts you were unprepared for at the time. But even though you cannot always know the content of future conflicts, you can prepare for likely scenarios and prepare for conflict in general. Whether it's a test, public speaking, driving, decision-making, getting married, or having children, preparation minimizes your level of fear when conflict hits.

Captain Torian said, "Preparation involves training for that environment—a specific combat situation. Set the expectations early. Prepare yourself for whatever the task is and study who did it before you. Learn from their shortcomings, so you don't fall into the same pitfalls." History is a great teacher when preparing for conflict, but we must be willing to learn from it. Preparation for any combat situation requires a leader to look to the past, consider the present, and secure what is needed for the future.

> *Preparation for any combat situation requires a leader to look to the past, consider the present, and secure what is needed for the future.*

Major Castaneda referred to this level of preparation as mental conditioning. For him, it began with a mentor, retired Marine Gunner CW05 Tim Gelinas, who served two tours in Vietnam, and later, one in Iraq. As a tactics and weapons expert, he informed Major Castaneda that "as a leader, when things start to go wrong, you will notice that everyone *below* you will suddenly have eyes *on* you." In these moments, leaders must maintain a mental discipline that controls mind, body, and spirit. This discipline will get leaders through the worst situations. As he described it, "You are aware of the dangers around you. If you panic, it becomes contagious, and you can hurt others. Leaders must maintain that mental value." This is true not only in military circles, but it is also true in your home, workplace, community, and the neighborhood where you live. As a leader, you will need mental conditioning to prepare for the fear associated with conflict.

Mental preparation requires a realistic type of training: practicing real situations where conflict occurs in a safe environment. Major Castaneda added that leaders need "resilience—a mental agility that can withstand the stress of an environmental factor. If not, you develop a 'fog of war,' where you can't disassociate what's happening in your body or environment because of what you are feeling. The hormone response to fear is powerful." Therefore, as we prepare to lead, and train others to lead, we must condition ourselves for situations we will encounter in the Combat Zone. He went on to say, "Settings with positive stress provide conditions that can shape or harden a person's mind, body, judgment, and, especially, their ethics." Preparation at this level is worth the effort for every leader in any situation and environment.

While interviewing Vice Admiral Bucchi about how he prepared for combat situations, he said, "What is important at the tactical level is that you have to know your own capabilities, strengths, and weaknesses. You also have to know the threat, who you are going against—their strong points and weak points." As he and I continued to discuss the necessity of preparation, he pointed out, "As a commanding officer, you take on a different leadership role. Now you have to learn how to take your individuals (those you lead) and pull them together as a unit. You have to show them how they are going to fit in a larger group of the organization." As he concluded the discussion, he said, "You have to be honest with what your capabilities are, you have to be honest with your weaknesses, and you have to be very conscious of the threat. How aggressive is that threat and how might that develop?" These thoughts emphasize the importance for all leaders to have a strong self-awareness, an ability to unite those they lead, and an awareness of how to deal with the stress that accompanies the challenges of leadership. To do so takes preparation.

In his book, *Moving Mountains: Lessons in Leadership and Logistics*, Lieutenant General William Pagonis describes a variety of areas related to leading in the Combat Zone as he recounts the lessons he learned from places like Vietnam's Mekong Delta and the Persian Gulf War. He led 40,000 men and women during the Persian Gulf War. In a Harvard Business Review article, Pagonis discussed the need for leaders to create and shape vision for a cooperative and collaborative environment, and he concluded that when it comes to preparation, "a key responsibility of the leader in building any organization that supports leadership is to educate."[36] When leaders combine realistic mental training with education, their preparation equips them to lead in the face of fear. Colonel Dorminey provided a summary of these thoughts, "Rise to the occasion or fall to your training (preparation). When under stress you rarely rise to the occasion…you typically fall to the level of training. It is therefore of the utmost importance to make the training of the highest caliber possible, realistic to the point that it induces similar stress of the real thing and then repeated until it becomes muscle memory. Then when the stress hits, you have a better feel how you will react, and the training can take over."

When leaders take steps to move out of the Comfort Zone, change is introduced. When those changes occur, conflict follows. The nature of the conflict will directly impact the decisions made for the organization moving forward. Realistic training in a safe environment and education are critical to making the type of decisions that assist you and your organization in working through the Combat Zone to a secure place. One fact that stood out from all these discussions, and summarized by Vice Admiral Bucchi, was the idea that leaders must recognize the need to be "fluid in their ability to go from being supported to a supporting commander back to being supported." The only way this happens is through preparation.

Know Yourself – Self-Evaluation

In his book, *The Art of War*, Sun Tzu said, "If you know the enemy and know yourself, you need not fear the result of a hundred battles. If you know yourself but not the enemy, for every victory gained you will also suffer a defeat. If you know neither the enemy nor yourself, you will succumb in every battle."[37]

Do you know who you are at your core? I cannot emphasize enough the importance of self-evaluation and introspection, especially when it comes to fear. Know what you fear. Ask yourself why you are afraid. Dig deeply into your past and see if something happened that led to this fear. Determine and write down your personal strengths and weaknesses. Every leader has limits, and you must learn how to adjust as the need arises. However, knowing yourself involves more than knowing your fears, strengths, and weaknesses.

A foundational step to leading any group, family, or organization begins with learning how to lead yourself. The only way to lead yourself is to know yourself. The ability to honestly evaluate who you are as a person, your core values, your ethical and moral compass, and your motive for leading all provide steps to leading yourself and leading through the Combat Zone. Feedback from others is valuable, but only when you can look at the person in the mirror and honestly deal with who you are will you master leading yourself. What is your purpose? Why do you lead? Why do you make the decisions you make? What are your priorities?

Leaders who know their "why" make decisions much more easily, because they learn what must be done today, right now. What are your core values? When your words and actions align with your core values, you never have to worry about consistency, because you operate with integrity. When followers notice inconsistency between your words and actions, they often lose confidence in your leadership in times of crisis.

How passionate are you about your work? I would rather work with someone whose abilities are weaker but has passion

> *There is no substitute for passion, and if you are leading without it, you may need to make a change.*

and a great attitude than work with someone who has incredible abilities but lacks passion and has a poor attitude. There is no substitute for passion, and if you are leading without it, you need to make a change. When you know who you are on the inside, what you are most passionate about, leading to a secure place occurs more quickly.

Know How Change Works

Understanding the nature of change and how it occurs makes all the difference in how you respond to fear. A glance at history over the last one hundred years highlights the incredible changes the world has experienced, from the Pony Express to the internet, from tin cans attached with a string to cell phones, from horse and carriage to fully electric automobiles, from telescopes to space exploration, and the list is unending. The changes experienced can be overwhelming to consider.

The nature of change and how change happens may not be as complicated as you might think. Seth Godin outlined three specific ways change happens.[38] The first is "slowly then all at once." On the surface, many of the changes I listed above seem to have occurred rapidly. However, many of these changes were developments that took decades to implement. As Godin said it, "Cultural change always happens relatively slowly. Person by person, conversation by conversation. Expectations are established, roles are defined, systems are built." These cultural shifts or changes occur slowly, then all at once.

Second, change can happen "from the foundation." People in the spotlight of the world tend to get most of the attention when it comes to change. In my research about presidents over the last century, I noticed as each decade passed, the definition of leadership changed. At times, the circumstances on a national and global scale influenced the definition. At other times, the type of leader serving as president influenced the definition. Either way, the change was rooted in the people who made up the culture. Godin points out, "We are the culture, and we change it or are changed by it." Knowing this fact should move leaders to understand that introducing any kind of change must occur at the foundational level first.

Third, Godin identifies that change happens "from peer to peer." The idea is that change happens horizontally. The daily conversations, expectations placed on one another, people who are followed, and the way in which we determine what is normal all directly impact change. He goes on to say, "People who are consistently and actively changing the culture are not easily distracted. One more small action, one more conversation, one more standard established." As one person influences change in another, the chain reaction that unfolds creates a spiderweb effect, which ultimately impacts the entire culture. Godin summarized with this thought, "If you care, keep talking. Keep acting. Stay focused. And don't get bored."

Fear can be detrimental to you and your organization. However, knowing how change works will assist you determine how to respond when fear exists. Whether slowly and then all at once to the horizontal nature of change, fear associated with change in the Combat Zone can be dealt with when we know how change works.

Establish Priorities

I am constantly amazed how much easier it is to move to a better Zone when my priorities are clear. Without priorities, it is easy be led around by fear. If there are no priorities, on what basis do you make decisions, and why would anyone care what decision you make? The inverse rings true as well: When you communicate priorities, not only are you guided in your decisions, but followers have greater confidence in you to lead. A friend of mine says, "Priorities are only valuable if they help you say *No*. If everything is a priority, then I say *No* to nothing, and the lack of focus dilutes the effort and little changes. But if I say *No* to low priorities in favor of higher one's, focus is maintained. If everything is a priority, then nothing is."

I've experienced times when there was so much work to be done, I didn't know where to start. I remember one specific situation when I was tasked to work with leaders in multiple locations internationally. When working for an international organization, you learn quickly that the world does not sleep, and neither will you at times. At one point, I found myself so overwhelmed I sat at my computer and stared at the screen. I felt nearly paralyzed from the weight of the responsibility and the demands of the workload. At that moment, a colleague walked into my office and asked about the situation. Once I explained, I remember his words. He asked, "What has to be done today? Focus only on what you *must* get done right now, in this moment, and then focus on the next need." Prioritizing my workload in this way increased my ability to deal with the pressure I felt and work through the demands more efficiently.

You must move beyond knowing who you are, how change works, leading yourself, and your motives for leading. Establishing priorities also requires you to know your followers and your organization. It's about knowing what is best for those impacted by your decisions. Instead of thinking about where people *want* to go, you first ask, where do they *need* to go?

Priorities can be characterized in four quadrants. Initially developed as the Eisenhower Matrix,[39] this design was intended to help distinguish between matters of urgency and importance. The following chart is one I created that has helped me.

Urgent - Important	Not Urgent - Important
Crises *Pressing problems* *Deadline-driven projects* *Meetings, preparations*	*Prevention / planning* *Exercise* *Relationship building* *Work-life balance*
Urgent - Not Important	Not Urgent - Not Important
Interruptions *Distractions* *Non-project emergencies* *Many popular activities*	*Trivia, busywork* *Gossip, idle speculation* *Pointless web-surfing* *Time wasters*

These four quadrants guide me in understanding how to establish the priorities that become foundational to every decision made. Your life and leadership may look different but prioritizing these areas will assist you in the journey to greater leadership. In an article about great leaders, Kara Goldin quotes former first lady Rosalyn Carter as having said, "A leader takes people where they want to go. A great leader takes people where they don't necessarily want to go, but ought to be."[40] Do you want to simply be a leader, or do you desire to be a great leader? Are you more concerned about the well-being of those you lead, or about yourself? The answer to these questions provides a basis for dealing with fear found that often accompanies conflict the Combat Zone.

Be Decisive

Making decisions is a key responsibility for any leader. Some decisions have little consequential value, such as daily routines that involve your route to the office, eating rituals, casual greetings, where office supplies are purchased, or answering the phone. However, there are other decisions that come with great consequence, such as designing budgets and allocating financial resources, recruiting and training employees, creating vision, strategic planning, or downsizing.

There are two types of decision-making structures within organizations: centralized and decentralized. The most traditional approach, found in older or smaller businesses, is the centralized structure, which primarily relies on a top-down decision-making process. The owner, CEO, top executive, or an executive team makes or approves every decision. The decentralized structure, an alternative found in many newer organizations, spreads the decision-making process throughout multiple levels. Usually, decisions are approved at lower levels and then reported to upper-level leaders. Both approaches are beneficial depending on the nature and makeup of the organization. Differences between these two structures include decision making speed, creation of standard internal metrics, relationships with customers, talent deployment, professional opportunities, definitive chain of command, and the flow of information.[41] As a leader, it is worth your time to examine the pros and cons of each to determine what works best within your organization.

Farnam Street Media created the Decision Matrix,[42] which, like the Eisenhower Matrix, categorizes the types of decisions leaders make. The Decision Matrix is designed to help leaders learn how and when to delegate decisions quickly. When accompanying the Eisenhour Matrix of priorities, the process can help leaders learn how to develop good judgment, critically think through consequential decisions that are irreversible, develop proper focus, and know when to use a team. The following chart provides a visual of the Decision Matrix.

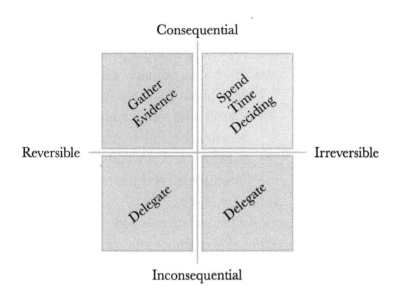

Consequential

Gather Evidence

Spend Time Deciding

Reversible — — — Irreversible

Delegate

Delegate

Inconsequential

Great leaders are known for being decisive. According to Sanjay Malhotra, there are four styles of decision-making.[43] The first is directive decision-making, which is done through a process of weighing out pros and cons to known situations. When the information is gathered and a clear *right* answer exists, directive decision-making is effective. The second is analytic decision-making, which requires a leader to thoroughly examine all information before acting. When there can be more than one right answer, leaders use their knowledge of the situation, observation, and consultation to determine the best course of action. The third is conceptual decision-making, which highlights a more social approach. This style involves more creative thinking and collaboration from multiple perspectives. When competing ideas and unpredictable circumstances exist, leaders provide a safe environment of experimentation to discover suitable solutions. The fourth style is behavioral decision-making, which ensures harmony in the working relationship among all involved. This style of decision-making presents possible solutions to the group and affords the group with an opportunity to weigh out the pros and cons to make the most effective decision.

Being decisive requires you to examine available data, compare the options, consider who the decision will affect,

> *Decision-making is never more critical than when encountering fear in the Combat Zone.*

think about the consequences, consult with others who have experienced similar decisions, and as Peter Drucker clearly stated, "decide what is right, rather than what is acceptable."[44] Decision-making is never more critical than when encountering fear in the Combat Zone. Therefore, it is essential to remember four thoughts.

Do not try to please everyone. You try. Even though you intellectually know it is not possible, you still try, and you try hard. If you experience the fear of someone leaving your organization, then you understand my point. You want your people to stay and be an active part of the organization. There is nothing wrong with wanting everyone to be active; but, when you do everything in your power to please everyone, the effects begin to weaken your influence and immobilize growth. I find it interesting that the people we try to please the most are often the farthest from us or those who are the hardest to please. In the process, we tend to push away people who have great ideas, but we are less concerned with pleasing, because we think they will always be around and close.

Sadly, the longer leaders foster this mindset, the more unaware of the practice they become. You also fail to realize the impact on your leadership and the overall health of the organization. Far too often, the loss that accompanies this practice is greater than the gain received from keeping a few people happy. You lose credibility when you are indecisive, and your organization remains stagnant.

Avoid the Squeaky Wheel Syndrome. Perhaps you are familiar with the saying, "The squeaky wheel gets the grease." As you drive, the wheels on your car roll along with no sound and the ride is smooth. However, if one of the wheels begins to make a noise (squeak), you know it needs attention, and, most likely, you will provide what is needed (grease). It is not uncommon that the remaining wheels receive no attention.

The phrase—an idiom or metaphor—indicates that the problem that is the loudest gets the most attention. The concept is quite simple. While it is not an absolute, in many situations (asking for a raise, getting a promotion, obtaining a discount, negotiating a decision, etc.) those who complain the most or speak up the loudest tend to be heard first. Sadly, this generally means that those who remain quiet, often refusing to speak up, go unheard and receive little or no attention.

In leadership, the Squeaky Wheel Syndrome occurs when decisions are heavily influenced by the one or two who create the most noise or disruption while everyone else remains silent. While there are circumstances where the noisiest problems deserve the most attention, those circumstances are not what I am talking about here. Squeaky wheels want you to know they have a problem and that something must be done immediately—specifically what *they* want done. Trying to please everyone and the Squeaky Wheel Syndrome go hand-in-hand in this regard, and they often lead to greater indecision.

Avoid indecision. Why do leaders often have such a hard time making decisions? It is likely that they are waiting on more information and trying to gather all the facts before deciding, which is a good trait. Col. Dorminey suggested, "Leaders (especially at the strategic level) can never get all the data. They often make decisions on partial data. In the military we talk about the only perfect intel is called history. So, you need to make decision often on partial or worse inaccurate data. I tell my subordinate leaders to make decisions on partial data when further delay waiting for more data would adversely impact their ability to execute the decision. I would rather them move out on a wrong decision and adjust than be paralyzed waiting for "perfect" intel." We may also find they don't want to make a decision because of the consequences. Knowing that a decision will disrupt the status quo, upset someone, offend those who don't like change, or cause a few to leave the organization is not a good enough reason to avoid making a decision. I will be the first in line to say that leaders should never *want* to disrupt, upset, offend, or cause anyone to leave. Furthermore, change for the sake of change is never fruitful. But to remain indecisive to avoid controversy or conflict in these areas will do more harm than good in the long run.

When a leader commits and follows through on their commitment, credibility increases.

Whatever the reason, you should know that not making a decision is a decision itself, which goes back to the consequences I mentioned previously. What if you make the wrong decision? When this happens, admit it, evaluate the situation, formulate a new approach, and decide again.

Learn the power of "yes" and "no". When faced with a decision, saying "yes" or "no" are your main options. There is the possibility of saying "wait until later," but the bottom line shows that at some point you must make a decision one way or another. Remaining neutral is not an option. I appreciate the integrity demonstrated by those who stick to their "yes." I even appreciate the value of a "no" for the same reason. When a leader commits and follows through on their commitment, credibility increases.

You possess incredible power with the use of both words. I once heard, "Every time you say *yes* to something, you say *no* to something else." You cannot say yes to everything. People that say "yes" to everything and everyone appear to be fake and lack integrity, as it is impossible to sustain the "yes man" lifestyle. At some point, it all breaks down. Learning how to say no at the right time opens you up to say yes to greater priorities in life. This is the reason vision plays a significant role in your leadership. When you have your vision in place you know when to say yes or no. Whatever helps you achieve your vision gets a yes, and whatever does not gets a no. This type of approach to decision-making limits the influences of other people's opinions and provides a more objective basis for your choices.

Lean On Others

More than one leader has crumbled under the weight of thinking they had to do it on their own. Leading on your own increases fear in your life and creates more conflict than you can handle. This may be one of the most difficult yet necessary suggestions to help you move toward success.

Leaning on others begins with due diligence. You must evaluate the situation for which you need help and research the right source from which help can be found. You can read books written on leadership or on the decision with which you're faced. You can lean on those who are more experienced leaders, which enables them to use their wisdom to guide you and opens a door to learn from those who have traveled a similar path. You can rely on members of your organization, delegating where necessary and seeking input from your constituents.

Numerous sources are available. It is up to you to locate and lean on them. The impact on your leadership is immeasurable.

The Combat Zone presents many challenges. Leadership is never more needed. Dr. Andrew Campbell writes, "The absence of leadership during uncertain, complex, and unpredictable times drives chaos, instability, and volatility in the environment."[45] The conflict encountered in this Zone can push a leader and their organization back into the Comfort Zone if the situation is not handled correctly. Campbell went on to say, "Leaders must give up the illusion of command and control, as well as accepting the comfort of being uncomfortable in this chaotic environment. The illusion of predictability in a global context is unattainable within a fluid and complex institutional and organizational environment." While you may want to avoid moving back into the Comfort Zone, you must also be careful not to allow yourself to enter more dangerous territory. As I will explore in the next chapter, the Danger Zone is an area where leaders far too often find themselves as a result of conflict.

In The Combat Zone

1. Which characteristics of the Combat Zone do you see in yourself, your organization's current leadership, or the organization overall?

   a. Change
   b. Conflict (forced or initiated)
   c. Insecurities
   d. Causalities
   e. Acceptance / Consensus
   f. Uncertainty and Unknown
   g. Lack of Trust

2. Describe changes implemented in the last 1-5 years for your organization.

3. What was the response to these changes?

4. When resistance occurred, would you describe the conflict as "forced" or "initiated"?

5. How did leadership respond to the conflict?

6. How open to receiving feedback are you as a leader in your organization?

7. On a scale of 1-5, describe the level of trust within the organization as it relates to the current leadership team.

1 ——————————— 3 ——————————— 5

Reactive	Neutral	Honest
Ineffective		Proactive
Non-Existent		Efficient

8. What changes can be made to foster trust in the organization's leadership?

Chapter Three

The Danger Zone

"Only those who will risk going too far can possibly find out
how far one can go."
T.S. Eliot

The anthem for the 1986 hit movie and its 2022 sequel, *Top Gun,* comes from the words in Kenny Loggins' song, "Danger Zone." The song and movie invite the observer into an area of risk, which is often life-threatening. Notice the bridge and last verse of the song:

> "You'll never say hello to you
> Until you get it on the red line overload
> You'll never know what you can do
> Until you get it up as high as you can go
>
> Out along the edges
> Always where I burn to be
> The further on the edge
> The hotter the intensity
>
> Highway to the Danger Zone
> Gonna take you right into the Danger Zone"[46]

Both movies highlight Maverick for his hotshot fighter pilot skills. In the original, Maverick's arrogant attitude, self-centered tendencies, recklessness, and willingness to take unnecessary risks create animosity between him and the other pilots, including Iceman, the antagonist of the movie. Maverick fails to value the team over his own individualism. After the loss of his close friend, Goose, Maverick learns several lessons about himself and his role as a pilot. As the plot unfolds, the greatest lesson he learns occurs in a fight with MiGs that outnumber him and archrival, Iceman. Maverick refuses to leave Iceman without a wingman, and as they fight to victory, they gain a newly formed admiration and respect for each other.

The risky and thrilling plot of *Top Gun* glamorizes the concept of the Danger Zone. But while danger and risk often go hand-in-hand, they are not synonymous in leadership. The Danger Zone I refer to here should be avoided. The qualities Maverick demonstrated—an arrogant attitude, self-centered tendencies, recklessness, and the willingness to take unnecessary risks—can also characterize your leadership when you enter the Danger Zone. When this happens, division and destruction loom on the horizon.

What is the Danger Zone?

The Danger Zone is a place where you will encounter many of your greatest challenges. Perhaps more so than in the Comfort Zone or the Combat Zone, it is critical that you learn to recognize when you're in the Danger Zone. The characteristics of this Zone are especially detrimental if you are unaware that you're in it. When you discover that you are headed into or are already in the Danger Zone, you must learn how to lead wisely. A failure to lead correctly can have grave consequences: a loss of credibility and trust, unwillingness on the part of others to follow, and ultimately, failure to reach the end goal. Addressing the characteristics of the Danger Zone is critical to get your leadership and organization back on the right track.

The Danger Zone is a frightening place for both you as a leader and those who follow. This Zone represents a place where you will struggle most in your ability to lead. You will be challenged as a leader because the characteristics of the Danger Zone act like a cancer that destroys you from the inside out and can destroy your leadership if not addressed. In this chapter, I will explore the characteristics of the Danger Zone. I will also provide suggestions on how to avoid and overcome each.

Apathy and Complacency

Few qualities present more danger than apathy and complacency. Perhaps you are familiar with the saying, "I couldn't care less." This expression reflects the mindset of apathy and complacency, and the effects when applied to your leadership are incalculable. When you reach a point that you do not care, destructive tendencies soon follow. While your leadership suffers on a personal level, the effect on everyone around you is also destructive. As an apathetic leader, you are present in body but have no presence with your team or organization. Any performance level becomes acceptable, regardless of how poor. Sadly, when you are apathetic or complacent, those who follow become uninterested and disengaged in their work. The impact on the bottom line of the organization is obvious.

> *When you are apathetic or complacent, those who follow become uninterested and disengaged in their work.*

In high school, I had instructors who made every effort to teach us the importance and value of working as a team. I understood the concept when it came to sports, but it did not always translate into the classroom. The instructor would often divide the class into groups and inform us that we would work together as a team, giving each team member specific responsibilities for the group project. To encourage equal contribution among team members, we were told that we would each receive the same grade upon completion of the project.

I do not need to reference one specific class, assignment, or project, because the result was the same. In *every* team I worked on in high school, one student—occasionally more than one—did not care about the project or grade. They were content with just passing the class, regardless of the outcome from the group assignment. Their apathy and complacency led to a lack of participation at team meetings and discussions. Of course, the effort they put forth to fulfill their responsibilities was nearly nonexistent.

The impact on each team was devastating. The domino effect was natural. Team members began to contact the apathetic member and urge them to help. As time to complete the project drew near, concern became panic and began to consume team members who actually cared about the assignment. Options were discussed. Responsibilities would either be divided among the remaining team players, or one member of the team would take on whatever was needed to finish. What we failed to learn at a young age was how to assign work within each member's passion or skill set, create ownership, and hold each other accountable. The stress and anxiety were unnecessary, but a reality all the same.

Apathy and complacency, even by one team member, create dangerous situations. When they exist among one or more leaders within the organization, the fallout is tragic. These two qualities produce discouragement and can lead to division, or worse…destruction. Obviously, the burden carried by the team becomes intense and increases the amount of fatigue experienced by all.

How can you avoid these destructive qualities and the danger they bring to your leadership, team, or organization? Here are five suggestions as a starting point for the discussion.

ALWAYS be self-aware. Observe your own behaviors and be aware of changes in the direction of your leadership that might be symptoms of apathy. Consider a self-assessment exercise. Make a comprehensive list of behaviors you recognize in others that concern you. Rank them by risk level and, in some cases, by category. Complete this exercise by asking yourself if you are currently demonstrating any of these behaviors. If you struggle with seeing these symptoms in yourself, work with a mentor outside the organization who will provide honest, candid, and a non-biased evaluation. This exercise will help you identify potential areas related to apathy.

Focus on your passion. Let me clarify that this does not mean you can eliminate ever working in areas you are less than passionate about. The nature of leadership involves working on specific tasks that are less than pleasurable. However, what this step does mean is that when you focus the majority of your time in areas where you are passionate, work becomes a joy, you feel more satisfied, and your influence on other team members or colleagues increases.

Conduct a 360-degree assessment. Talk with the people on your team, above and below you, and listen to their feedback. Identify any potential behavioral signs of apathy. Conducting regular assessments can provide valuable information with which to evaluate your attitude and ability. It may be necessary to obtain information through anonymous surveys, 3rd party surveys, or other means to encourage and maintain a level of privacy.

Communicate. Do not be afraid to communicate the challenges that animate your apathy at its core. The ability to speak openly about these struggles can help immeasurably. Encourage others to do the same. If you think you are communicating enough, you probably aren't.

Help others. When you notice the same signs in other employees or members of the team, talk to them and help them work through the symptoms. Provide encouragement and be present with them. When you help others, you ultimately help yourself grow and overcome the dangers of apathy and complacency.

Promote ownership. Doug Dickerson suggests promoting ownership, developing community, and creating a culture that understands why you work together as community.[47] Holding each other accountable through the promotion of ownership increases an awareness of apathy and complacency and affords you an opportunity to implement the tools to overcome the effects of both.

Overconfidence

Overconfidence and apathy may appear as opposites, but in the Danger Zone, they often produce the same results. One who is apathetic may stop questioning their practices, causing them to believe too strongly in their own methods and abilities. While confidence is a great quality to possess, overconfidence is often foundational to pride and arrogance. During my high school basketball career, I experienced highs and lows. I played power-forward for the Mammoth Spring Bears. Our coach, Jack Haney, had an amazing reputation in the area, and he was tough. Like most athletes, my teammates and I did not enjoy the conditioning exercises at the end of practice. If the truth be told, we really didn't care much for practice at all. We loved to play the game. It would take a bit of maturity before I realized the futility of such thinking.

The team held an amazing record (23-4) as we headed into the district regional tournament during my senior year. Our record was better than any previous team the school had seen in nearly twenty years. We had already scored a great victory in the local Tri-County Tournament, where we defeated one of the best teams in the state. I still remember the words of Coach

Haney as he walked into the locker room after cutting down the net: "Boys, victory is sweet!" Yes, coach, it is sweet. Over forty years later, I recall that victory with pride and excitement.

We were favored to win the district regional tournament, and we were pumped about heading to the state tournament. We won the first two games with little difficulty. We were confident—maybe a bit overconfident. As we approached the semi-final game, we were scheduled to play against a team from Cloverbend, a town smaller than Mammoth Spring. In fact, one might more accurately refer to Cloverbend as a "spot in the road." If you blinked, you missed it, even if you knew where it was. Did I mention we were confident?

I am certain you have surmised the outcome by now. It was ugly—*really* ugly. As I heard growing up, we "couldn't hit the broad side of a barn." We missed easy shots, made senseless turnovers, developed foul trouble early, and watched in misery as Cloverbend defeated us and went on to win the tournament and make their way to State. We learned long-lasting lessons that night. While we ended the season with a record of twenty-five wins and only five losses, the final loss was what we remembered most. I am sure the entire team would love to return to that night and play the game one more time.

In much the same way, when overconfidence leads to pride and arrogance in your leadership, destructive challenges follow. The moment you begin to think you can do it on your own or develop the "I got this" type of thinking, you begin ignoring wise counsel and refusing to seek help. That's when you know the problems of pride and arrogance associated with overconfidence are taking hold. Major Castaneda said the most important thing for a leader is to know "they *do not* have all the answers." He went on to add this thought: "The worst thing is to follow someone who has all the

> *The most important thing for a leader is to know they **do not** have all the answers.*

answers but won't listen to anyone." The danger that accompanies this type of arrogance can destroy your credibility, costing you the respect of others within the organization. Worse still is the possibility of leading the organization to failure or causing its closure. How can you avoid these dangers?

Find a mentor. Good mentors have a way of keeping you humble. Their honest feedback can help you learn not to think more highly of yourself than you should. A friend of mine once said that our biggest challenge is seen in that we usually judge ourselves by our intentions. However, others judge us by our actions. Effective mentors have a way of keeping everything in the right perspective and providing unbiased counsel. They help align our intentions and actions to provide others with an accurate picture of our leadership.

Evaluate the criticism of others. The ability to listen to criticism without being defensive is an immeasurable gift. You can recognize the depth of overconfidence when you find yourself becoming defensive when criticized. Stop, step back, and ask yourself, is there any value in the criticism? If the answer is yes, then learn how to accept the criticism graciously by saying, "thank you," and potentially asking for help in how to improve. The humility expressed by this conduct will raise your credibility as a leader.

Be a learning leader. Few qualities will help you more as a leader than being a perpetual student. Always be open to learn from others. The most effective leaders are notably the best learners. You will increase your ability to lead, know how to remain humble, avoid becoming overconfident, and develop your best self as a learning leader. Pick up a book, talk to others who lead, listen to those you lead, pay attention to world events, and reflect on the actions and results from historical leaders.

Col. Dorminey talked about the need for critical self-analysis, "Even when things go well but especially when they don't, most people find it easy to find blame in others. A learning leader will always start with themselves and own the failure, debrief what went wrong, seek a root cause of what they, as the leader, did to cause or contribute to the failure and learn from it." The benefit of critical self-analysis as a learning leader will strengthen your leadership quickly.

Prepare appropriately. Closely associated with being a learning leader is the idea of preparation. As I have already identified, preparation is essential at every level of leadership. When you take time to adequately prepare, you experience an appropriate level of confidence. You need confidence when leading, but you must also avoid the pitfalls that accompany overconfidence. The difference is preparing appropriately. Know what needs to be done to either avoid the Danger Zone or move through it. Once you know the direction, prepare yourself and others. The confidence created will build momentum and keep you grounded as a team.

The Danger Zone is never more prevalent than when you are overconfident. When you refuse to listen to the counsel of others, are unaware of current trends within organizational culture, and continue to push a methodology or approach that is archaic and irrelevant to clientele's demands, you may be suffering from overconfidence.

Stress

I've already mentioned "stress and anxiety," but I want to dig more deeply into the danger caused by stress. The challenges that arise when leaders face crises or conflict increase the level of stress to a degree that often moves leaders into the Danger Zone. The dangers associated with these stressful times bring severe consequences. Medical experts have long emphasized the physical and emotional consequences related to stress: high blood pressure, heart disease, obesity, diabetes, lower immune system, low energy, frustration, moodiness, feeling overwhelmed, anger, social anxiety, depression, and addictive tendencies. When you deal with this kind of stress, as the song indicates, you are pushing it to the "red line overload." The outcome has a major impact on your ability to lead and the willingness of others to follow.

You may not always be able to eliminate or avoid stress in your life, because stress can hit you from any and every angle: at home, on the job, and in your community. Sometimes, a simple drive home from the office can leave you feeling stressed. If you live in a larger city, you know exactly what I mean. You can, however, take a few steps to reduce the level of stress in your life. Consider a few simple starting points:

Exercise. For starters, physicians are the first to suggest exercise as a primary way to deal with stress. Even if it is going for a walk, taking time for exercise works to reduce the level of stress you may experience.

Eat better. Diet changes also help reduce stress. If you are a Red Bull, Monster, or five-cups-of-coffee kind of person, eliminating that level of caffeine might be helpful. Additional changes to the types of foods you eat can also provide support for reducing stress, such as reducing your consumption of foods that slow you down. Eat out less; eat at home more.

Create more family time. Spend time with family or friends or engage in an activity you find relaxing (and don't say "work" here). While you might believe work relaxes you, the idea is to take time away from the areas creating stress and focus on something or someone that provides a bit of respite.

Be transparent. Transparency in your life, whether at work or home, can reduce stress. *If you are the type of person that keeps secrets from your family, friends, or colleagues, there is a good chance you are dealing with undue stress.* Be more open and communicate, even if it is difficult at first. Taking these steps will help. Your mental and physical health may depend on it.

Disconnect. A great practice for all leaders involves disconnecting from electronic devices. If you want to improve your mental health and reduce stress, learning to turn off your devices will go far. Set appropriate boundaries. You may want to start with something as simple as setting your cell phone in another room during family dinners each night. Stay focused and be present with your family. The benefit is immeasurable to your overall health and stress level.

Say NO. Learn how to say no graciously. You may need to start slow and build up, but this is a very important skill in the long run. I am not the best at this one, but I am improving. I can empathize with the impulse to take on too much: I want to help others, and I like the feeling I get when I say yes to someone who has a need. However, when you find yourself saying yes to everything, before long, you have no time to accomplish all you've committed to at work or home. Protect your time as much as possible.

Meditate or practice deep breathing. Various forms of meditation or the practice of deep breathing are also helpful. Learning to calm your body and mind by observing your surroundings (sights, sounds, and smells), closing your eyes to relax and focus on your attitude as it relates to a specific situation, or through breathing deeply for a few minutes makes a significant difference in a stressful situation.

Think positively. We are constantly surrounded with negativity. Negative thinking increases your level of stress. However, learning to develop a more positive focus reduces it. The Mayo Clinic published an article with the benefits of positive thinking. Among the many physical benefits, the article suggests that positive thinking lowers the rate of depression and provides better coping skills during hardships and times of stress.[48]

Find a practice that works for you and use it, because you must deal with stress. If you don't find ways to reduce stress, the repercussions can be life-threatening. Along with the physical and mental consequences that accompany stress, failing to address those stressors in your life will leave you fatigued to the point of exhaustion.

Exhaustion and Burnout

One of the biggest challenges the Danger Zone presents is exhaustion. When leaders reach a point where they feel they cannot continue to do the job, it is not uncommon to hear them reference being burned out. I do not question the fact that you are tired. With all that's happening in the world—from years of dealing with a pandemic to the economic effects of the Russia-Ukraine conflict—it is only natural that you would feel fatigue. However, this fatigue does not have to lead to burnout. In fact, burnout is a more complex concept than you might think.

The term "burnout" is connected to stress in the workplace that has not been managed properly or successfully. The feelings of depletion, cynicism, and mental distancing from the job associated with burnout are the result of exhaustion. When exhaustion occurs, you experience at least three major changes that impact your leadership: depleted decision-making skills, mood swings, and suspicion.

When you are exhausted, your ability to make wise and timely decisions suffers. The discomfort that accompanies conflict, which often leads to the Danger Zone, keeps you from thinking clearly. The mind is cloudy, distracted from the numerous responsibilities associated with family and work. Because frustration is a bedfellow to exhaustion, decisions that normally require a few seconds to make now take more time. The result is increased frustration, forcing you to attempt making decisions that feel rushed, which often leads to undesirable results. These rash decisions not only impact your leadership, but they often hurt others around you.

> *When you are exhausted, your ability to make wise and timely decisions suffers.*

Exhaustion changes your mood. The analogy of a "short fuse" is fitting when you get tired. This quick-to-anger spell hits home with family and coworkers. It seems that even the smallest things that don't go your way can set you off, even though you would not react the same way under normal circumstances. When you are tired, you do not think the same way you normally do. Thus, you come across like the Hulk: you are angry all the time and it doesn't take much provocation for you to become green, ugly, and destructive. The atmosphere created by these mood swings causes everyone to live in fear and resentment, which is not good for your leadership.

Your level of suspicion also rises when you are fatigued. You become suspicious of just about everyone and everything. You wonder if others are against you. You question motives, even when the intent is clearly pure. You doubt the sincerity of any gesture or act of kindness, and you respond with an attitude of contempt. You perceive that others are taking advantage of you. Of course, you cannot allow this to happen, so you take corrective measures to ensure that others know you are aware of their ploy, even if your assessment is wrong (as it often is in the face of exhaustion). This is where pride cycles back into the equation.

Exhaustion can be avoided in the Danger Zone, but there is no list of steps. I do not individually address the changes in your character that are associated with exhaustion, because what you need is simply to rest. You must make time to let the mind and body recover. Remember, there is a difference in *finding* time to rest and *making* time to rest. From a leadership perspective, rest must start at the top and work its way down. Few organizations encourage employees to rest. Productivity has become dependent on not resting which, in my opinion, often decreases productivity. It is one thing to encourage people to rest, but it is another to give them time to rest or pay them while they enjoy time off. I recently heard it expressed this way: "Well rested happy people are very hard to discourage." Consider the value

> *"Well rested happy people are very hard to discourage."*

of that to your organization. While you may often think you don't have time to get the rest you need, without the proper amount of rest, you'll only dive deeper into the Danger Zone.

Discouragement

Nothing destroys your leadership or organization more quickly than discouragement. Many of the previously discussed characteristics of the Danger Zone lead to discouragement. When people are stressed and wrestling with fatigue, discouragement will soon follow. Frustration in your home, on the job, with other leaders, or with the direction of the country fuels discouragement. Fear that surfaces because of uncertainty with your job, instability in your family, or the unknown promotes discouragement. Dwelling on past failures as a spouse or parent, an employer or employee, or maybe on a personal level push you toward discouragement. You may constantly be bombarded with everything from the unexpected to the unbelievable, and when it happens, you are forced to decide how to respond. Too many fall into the trap of allowing discouragement to overtake them. This response is destructive, especially for leaders.

When you experience discouragement, the future looks dim. If the discouragement is great enough, your first thought is to quit. You lose all hope of your situation improving. The easy answer is to give up and try something else, or just try to disappear. As I consulted leaders from different types of organizations over the course of the pandemic, one common theme continued to surface: They were discouraged, and it continues. For many of them, this was the most difficult season in the history of leading their organizations. Decisions had to be made to comply with CDC guidelines, which often divided people within their organizations. Regardless of the decision, it never seemed to be more than 50% right. Weeks dragged into months, which dragged into years, dealing with these issues. It discouraged leaders across the board.

When organizations are led by discouraged leaders, people tend to respond with a sequence of four reactions. First, they begin to question the vision and mission of the organization. They ask, "Are we really headed in the right direction? Do leaders know where we are going?" Second, they become suspicious of every decision. The plans did not work, and the goals seem unreachable, so people begin to question why they should try anymore. They wonder, "Is it worth the effort?" Third, they begin to distrust everyone. They are skeptical of the leadership and their coworkers. They no longer trust leaders to steer them in the right direction. Sadly, this distrust impacts their performance. And fourth, they reject their leaders. As a final step, and perhaps the worst possible outcome, people rebel. They will not put up with this type of leadership any longer. They strike (personally or as part of a group), or they just leave.

I've been discouraged at times throughout my life. I have been disheartened within family, work, projects, plans, expectations, and the list goes on. I am sure you have been discouraged in some or all of these areas at one point or another. Regardless of the individual or situation, it is important to take a proactive approach to overcoming discouragement. The following list provides a few possibilities.

Label it. Step back and just call it what it is. Self-awareness and acknowledgement are a starting point to help you overcome discouragement. Say it out loud: "I am discouraged. I am disappointed this did not go the way I wanted it to go." For me, this is a good first step.

Get some perspective. Take a moment to put the situation in proper perspective. Some situations can be far more difficult than others. Framing it within the right perspective can help you understand more clearly how to deal with the situation. Another option that may help you see the situation more clearly is to ask someone familiar with the circumstances for their perspective. Fresh eyes can usually provide a better view. Malcolm Gladwell in his book *David and Goliath,* talks about how we are discouraged because of the "giant" issue in front of us and in reality, we've made the issue bigger than it is. Perspective helps us size up the problem rationally rather than emotionally.[49]

Start something new. This may take the form of a new vision, new goals, new plans, new projects, etc. Starting something new provides a little extra excitement, perhaps incentive or motivation, and can often help address the discouragement from previous events.

Celebrate progress. Please do not wait until something big happens or is accomplished before celebrating. For me, I love a bowl of ice cream to celebrate a good day of writing. Pick something small but sweet to help you celebrate each little accomplishment. This will give you something to look forward to each day.

Avoid emotional vampires. I am sure you know people who somehow possess the ability to suck the life out of every positive moment. They tend to become the Negative Nancy and Defeatist Dan for every situation. Since misery loves company, they work hard to recruit others to adopt their mindset. Don't allow yourself to fall into their trap. Learn how to recognize these individuals, be cautious around them, or find ways to avoid them altogether if possible.

Find a Barnabas. Everyone needs a Barnabas in their life. The name Barnabas means "Son of Encouragement," which is why the biblical character Barnabas received this name. When you have an encourager in your life and you start feeling discouraged, call them up and take them to lunch. Before you know it, you may start to see the bright side of your situation or gain a new spark of motivation.

Choose encouragement. When you find yourself feeling discouraged, know you are not alone. To be totally honest, discouragement is a *choice* you make about how you approach the situations you encounter. If you really want to overcome your own discouragement, take time to help someone else overcome theirs. Encourage as many people as possible. It doesn't take as much effort as you might think. Doing so takes the focus off yourself and places it on others, and when this happens, the serotonin flows and contributes to more positive emotions.

I have experienced the negative effects of discouragement at various times in my life, as I am sure you have also. You have probably seen the results in political, corporate, civil, and religious organizations. Overcoming discouragement is vital to the success of your leadership.

Relational Tension

A major consequence of the Danger Zone is relational tension. While this tension is often the result of exhaustion during times of high stress, it can occur at any moment during conflict. In the twenty-first century, the world has experienced many major conflicts, each causing relational tension. These events changed the way we travel, the way we approach organizational strategy and planning, and even how we interact with others.

One of the first events was the terrorist attacks of 9/11. The collapse of the twin towers, the airplane crash in a Pennsylvania field, and the airplane crash into the Pentagon unfolded in a matter of hours. The country was paralyzed by television reports as the horrifying images were replayed over and over. The result was an international dilemma with which the world continues to grapple more than twenty years later. The global war on terrorism associated with 9/11 has manifested in relational tension between countries around the world. This tension plays a central role on the world stage, as conflict continues to rage between countries over the rising insurgents among developing nations. An international conflict is not unique to the war on terrorism; for example, Russia's invasion of Ukraine also raised tensions and impacted intercultural relationships on a global scale.

Another event that catapulted relational tension to a new level was the introduction of COVID-19. The pandemic ushered in a period of conflict that affected every person on the planet. The tension divided the United States and the world over masks, vaccinations, international travel, and more. The political environment is not the only area of life in which relational tension rose because of this pandemic. Families, businesses, churches, social circles, and the scientific community, among others can be added to the long list of groups impacted by relational tension. The tension became so heated that division continues to impact each of us. Both sides of these debates are passionate, and unity on the issue seems unlikely.

Where does it all leave us? The Danger Zone exists because leaders are uncertain as to what decisions should be made. Relational tension impacts your leadership and your relationships with those who follow. Is it possible to address this tension in ways that help you move out of the Danger Zone? Explore a few suggestions with me.

Know the stress points. Usually, though not always, tension is a symptom of a greater underlying problem or source of conflict. Col. Dorminey identified mission focus as the key, "I've got multiple examples of infighting among my airmen even when things were relatively good. Then this same group is humming along like a well-oiled machine in austere locations under significant stress only a few days later. The difference… mission focus." Know your own personal stress points and address them. If you can, learn the stress points of others in your organization as well, so that you can sensibly and sensitively approach the issues. When you put yourself on the other person's side of the table and work to understand why they have these specific stress points, it will guide the conversation to more successful resolutions.

Avoid anger. When you try to resolve relational tension while angry, you rarely, if ever, succeed. In these heated moments, anger makes it difficult to listen clearly to the other person and it becomes easy to say things you later wish you could take back. Angry, ineffective communication does not promote resolution. When you feel angry, take time to back off and cool down. Think through the situation and approach the discussion with a calm spirit, ready to listen.

Sleep on it. When you are tired, small changes in "normal" circumstances can quickly become larger-than-life scenarios and the tension that accompanies these situations grows proportionately. Learn to rest. If the problem and tension continue after rest, then additional effort may be needed to resolve it. I realize there are situations that require immediate attention, so handle those accordingly. If you are tired, then take a night to rest and look at it through fresh eyes in the morning. You will be surprised how rest can give you a new perspective.

Look to yourself *first*. Relational tension usually exists because you feel someone has overstepped a boundary in the relationship. From your perspective, they did not do right by you. This may or may not be correct. However, if you can examine yourself, consider what really happened, the way it makes you feel about the situation and the other person involved, and the connection to your identity, the conversation that follows may look a bit different.

Adjust the vocabulary. Know when to say "I" instead of "you." Everyone makes mistakes. You need to stop for a moment and ask, "How have I contributed to this situation?"

When you think in terms of "I" instead of "you," then you are taking a huge step down the path of improving relationships with others. Learning to use "we" adds to success. Together, we will solve this problem or address this situation.

Create psychological comfort and safety. I first heard this concept in a podcast with retired FBI investigator, Joe Navarro. His book, *Be Exceptional*, discusses the need for psychological comfort—a place where everyone feels safe to express themselves without fear of punishment or humiliation.[50] Professor of Leadership at Harvard Business School and bestselling author, Amy Edmundson, writes, "In short, psychological safety is a crucial source of value creation in organizations operating in a complex, changing environment."[51] In other words, do your followers feel safe to ask questions, raise new ideas, challenge the status quo, speak truth to those in power, or admit a mistake? Major Castaneda added, "How leaders behave when they receive information determines how much people are willing to share. If a leader gets angry or 'kills the messenger,' people withhold news unless it's good." When you create a safe space, relational tension begins to resolve itself, and in some cases, it can be avoided altogether.

> *Leadership is built on relationships. The only way to successfully develop others in reaching their potential is through building the kind of relationships that promote growth.*

Leadership is built on relationships. The only way to successfully develop others in reaching their potential is through building the kind of relationships that promote growth. In his book, *The Multiplication Effect,* Mac Lake claims, "Programs don't develop leaders, leaders develop leaders. Leadership development is not a class you take, it's an intentional relationship you build."[52] The challenge you face in the Danger Zone is keeping those relationships secure. Doing so will strengthen your influence as a leader.

Losing Sight of the Vision

Another consequence of the Danger Zone, and one of the most dangerous, is losing sight of the vision. Staying focused on the vision is critical, and it is the driving force for any organization. The moment you lose sight of the vision, you become quickly entrenched in the Danger Zone. Without vision, people wander around trying to determine who they are and where they are headed. Consequently, when you lose sight of the vision as a leader, each layer in the Danger Zone intensifies, because there is no guiding light to move everyone ahead as a unified group.

Forced conflict is where you first struggle with keeping your eye on the vision. When conflict is unexpected and you are unprepared for it, you begin scrambling to determine what should be done. Situations like the examples discussed in the high risk/low frequency section of chapter 1 enter the picture, and the consequences of rash decisions can be destructive. Organizations in every sector are equally affected by forced conflict. While the reasons are numerous and complex, the lack of vision or losing sight of the vision is a primary factor. Depending on the intensity of the resistance, even initiated conflict can push you into the Danger Zone. Therefore, focusing on the vision is essential for leading through each Zone.

The unprecedented challenges that have persisted in recent years did not bring failure and loss for every organization. Many companies like DoorDash, HelloFresh, Amazon, Waiter.com, Uber Eats, and Grubhub, looked to the future regardless of the current reality and led their organizations to greater opportunities for growth and improvement. Instead of being consumed by the unknown and the potential for setbacks, they shifted their thinking toward stronger leadership and widening the scope of their influence to improve their current circumstances. These leaders and organizations were rare, but they raised the potential of each person in their organization, and although they faced the same crisis as everyone else, they found a way to be more successful than anybody would have thought possible. How did they do it? Vision! How can you keep your focus on the vision?

Prioritize. As I've already mentioned, nothing is more urgent in a crisis than knowing your priorities. Interestingly, self-preservation often becomes priority one. While I understand, I am concerned with how quickly leaders and organizations lose sight of their vision. When you stop to recalibrate and focus on your vision, decisions for moving through any crisis become clearer. Prioritize accordingly.

Minimize distractions. Determining distractions for each organization is subjective. What may present itself as a distraction in one area may not be the same for another. Some distractions, however, are fairly consistent, such as texts, phone calls, email, social media apps, etc. The world is constantly steeped in the dilemma of time management within the social media age. A quick glance at Facebook, Instagram, Twitter, or any of a hundred other apps can quickly turn into hours each day surfing through post after post. Not all distractions can be removed, but when you work to minimize those distractions, the focus strengthens. You also prioritize and manage time more wisely.

> *Not all distractions can be removed, but when you work to minimize those distractions, the focus strengthens.*

Manage your time wisely. As I mentioned in Chapter 2, Eisenhower's Time Management Matrix can help you decide where to allocate your time.[53] This matrix categorizes the urgency and importance of various activities and situations. But even if the Time Management Matrix is not right for you, a host of tools are available online to assist you in managing your time more appropriately. Your ability to manage time is directly related to the priorities you establish in your leadership.

OVER-Communicate expectations. In times of crises, communication is premium. Learning what to communicate during these times is crucial and will help you learn how, when, and what to communicate in the future to avoid suffering at the hands of similar events. In the Danger Zone, when you feel the stress of leadership, experience fatigue, and struggle with tension in relationships, learn to *over*-communicate clear expectations. Everyone needs to know what you expect from them as a leader, who is responsible for specific actions, when it needs to be completed, how each step is organized, and why their role is essential to move through this Zone. The expectations communicated by you are valued most during these times. These expectations must be directly linked to the vision and how the vision will be reached through those who follow.

Review daily. Although it is the final step in this list, review is no less important than the other suggestions for maintaining sight of your vision. The best way to stay focused on the vision is to review it daily. Remind yourself as a leader and remind your organization of the vision every day. Then evaluate your performance in living up to that vision.

You must recognize the possibility of danger, and instead of reacting, act. Stay focused on the vision. You must see the danger and act quickly. Weigh out every option and make the necessary decisions to push forward. Lead from the front and not the board room. Point everyone to the vision. All crises produce a host of variables to be considered, and when crisis strikes, you must step up to the leadership plate.

Sideline Leadership

The final characteristic of the Danger Zone is one that depicts you more as a spectator. You no longer lead from the front, cast the vision, or provide an example for others to follow. The temptation when conflict arises is to find a quick and easy solution, but quick and easy rarely, if ever, work in the long run. Most people do not like conflict. The thought of confrontation is frightening, which is why you cannot be known for beating around the bush, attempting to sweep things under the rug, speaking in generalities, or addressing everyone in the room about the problem hoping *the* one person who needs to change will catch on. There are times you will do anything and everything to avoid directly speaking to the individual who needs to be addressed. This may seem like an easy path, but remember the proverb, "Following the path of least resistance makes both rivers and men crooked."

The conflict experienced in the Combat Zone challenges the core of your leadership. If you are not careful, the conflict can take you out of the front and to the side or rear of the organization. This is a sign that you've left the Combat Zone and entered the Danger Zone. You will be tempted to pass down decisions from the board room without conducting the due diligence to know if it is the right decision. It is just quick and easy. Sadly, it can also come at a horrible cost to your leadership and the organization.

As a sideline leader, you will be shackled by your own pride. You become convinced that everything is running smoothly. The company does not need to worry about making any changes. You focus on and become diligent in maintaining the status quo. When challenged, you are quick to respond, "This is how we've always done it. It worked in the past and it will work now." As the external environment changes, a sideline leader is unable or unwilling to see the need to adjust organizational objectives to accommodate the new reality. Instead, they hold on to the notion that if they persevere, everything will return to normal, and it will be business as usual. The problem with this way of thinking is the fact that everything has changed. The playing field is different now. Avoiding the sideline can be difficult, but here are few ideas to prevent it.

Know your limitations. You cannot do it all, and attempting to do so leads to frustration and burnout. Know your strengths and weaknesses. Knowing your limits and leading within them will encourage all who follow. With a little introspection, you can practice your own abilities safely and promote greater growth within the organization.

Lead with honesty. It goes without saying, but honesty is foundational to leading. If you are found to be dishonest, followers will not trust or follow you. As a leader, learn to be honest about everything. When asked about the number one quality of a leader, Col. Dorminey said, "*authenticity*. Be honest about the situation and what you do know and what you don't." When your followers ask questions, do not hesitate to be honest about the situation and provide all the information *you can*. I realize not all information can be shared but being evasive only leads to concern and skepticism.

Find your purpose. I highly recommend Simon Sinek's book *Start with Why*.[54] As Sinek points out, good organizations know *what* to do and *how* to do it. But, great organizations understand *why*. Knowing the *why* behind your leadership provides you and your organization with focus and stability. When you are driven by purpose, you know why you cannot become complacent and lead from the sideline. As a friend of mine told me in a text, "On purpose, for a purpose." You must provide direction—the kind of direction centered on your *why*.

Communicate. I talk a lot, and I mean *a lot*, about communication in this book. I hope by the time you finish reading it, you will understand why. When you provide a place for safe and healthy communication, people will follow. They will feel more comfortable opening up about how to improve and move forward. Lead from the front by showing that you value what each person contributes to the organization. Give them a voice.

Provide support. In every leadership development model, you must provide support that sets people up for success. A leader's role is more about clearing the way for others to carry out the mission, than doing the mission. Once appropriate expectations are clearly presented, there must be systems in place that not only allow people to meet expectations, but also promote opportunities to be successful. What those systems look like will vary from one organization to the next. However, support structures will increase productivity and create greater leadership for the future.

Be creative. Great leaders promote creativity. I will be the first to say that my creativity gene is lacking. However, I know that when I surround myself with those who are creative, amazing things happen. I am always encouraged and impressed by creative thinkers and designers. If you want to grow as a leader and avoid the sidelines, open the door to those with creative abilities and give them the green light to use their gifts.

The Danger Zone is not easy to avoid. Sadly, you can dive into the Danger Zone at any point along the journey. It doesn't always take conflict to push you into dangerous territory. Being comfortable with the status quo is a danger in itself. Achieving success at the end of the journey can also create pride, which can lead to the Danger Zone if left unchecked.

On a factual level, most leaders will end up in the Danger Zone at one point or another. The key is to quickly identify when you are there and take action to get out. You must prepare and be aware of the danger that surrounds you to minimize the consequences of this Zone. When you find yourself in the Danger Zone, take the necessary steps to move out of it and into a safer place.

One last thought: the Danger Zone may happen, regardless of your preparation. However, the key is to minimize the depth and amount of time you spend in this Zone. Your level of preparation will help you get through it. Ultimately, you desire to lead your organization through the Combat Zone to the End Zone. As I will explore in the next chapter, while not the final step in the journey, the End Zone is the desired outcome that allows you to prepare for leading through future cycles of comfort, combat, and danger.

In The Danger Zone

1. Which characteristics in the Danger Zone do you see in your organization's current leadership?

   a. Apathy and Complacency
   b. Overconfidence
   c. Stress
   d. Exhaustion and Burnout
   e. Discouragement
   f. Relational Tension
   g. Losing Sight of the Vision
   h. Sideline Leadership

2. On a scale of 1 –5, how would you describe the current mindset of the leadership in your organization?

Apathetic	1 — 5	Engaged/Passionate
Overconfident	1 — 5	Confident/cautious
Stressed	1 — 5	Settled/peaceful
Exhausted	1 — 5	Energetic/resolute
Discouraged	1 — 5	Encouraged/encouraging
Sideline leader	1 — 5	Leading from front
No vision	1 — 5	Visionary

3. How do you typically handle expressions of dissatisfaction?

4. What avenues are provided to communicate and appropriately address frustration and discouragement?

5. On a scale of 1 – 5, how would you describe the atmosphere in the day-to-day operations of the organization?

Low energy	1 — 5	Interesting/exciting
Overconfident	1 — 5	Confident
Stressful	1 — 5	Peaceful
Exhausting	1 — 5	Energetic/efficient
Discouraging	1 — 5	Encouraging
Sideline leader	1 — 5	Leading from front
Skeptical/Frustrating	1 — 5	Bought in/driven

6. What changes would you make to assist leadership in addressing the Danger Zone and help move others in the organization from a 1 up to a 5?

Chapter Four

The End Zone

"People will rise to meet seemingly insurmountable obstacles and challenges if they understand the worthiness of the personal sacrifices and effort. Supporting that understanding must be mentors who provide leadership; without both ingredients, a cause will go unrealized and a mission is likely to fail."
Glenn R. Jones

The world seems to thrive on the game. The game may occur across the table, on a field or court, in an arena, or outdoors. Participants play for pleasure or livelihood, for the simple joy of playing, or when the stakes are high—at times, even when the game is a matter of life and death. People discipline their lives physically, mentally, emotionally, and spiritually in preparation for the challenges faced during competition. They develop greater focus and drive to give their best and beyond. From the peak of Mount Everest to the depths of the ocean and everywhere in between, men and women push themselves to succeed, even if the only things they compete against are themselves and the elements.

ABC's Wide World of Sports launched in 1961, and Jim McKay delivered one of the most famous introductory lines in sports history: "The thrill of victory and the agony of defeat. The human drama of athletic competition."[55] Anyone who has participated in sports or loves to watch a game knows the significance of his words. Whether we relive the glory days of our athletic and youthful abilities, fancy the style of an armchair quarterback, provide our commentary about poor officiating, or simply enjoy watching the contest, most people in our world connect with a game.

Our love for sport begins early in life, as parents encourage their children to compete in soccer, T-Ball, Little

League baseball, lil' dribblers basketball, flag football, dance, BMX, or any other extra-curricular activity. As children reach high school, sports become a little more intense. By the time they reach university level, the pool of athletes decreases, but the intensity increases. The rare few who become professional athletes speak about the mounting need for greater strength, speed, and agility to achieve success.

To witness the cultural importance of sports, one needs to look no further than the role of football in American society. American football originated in the mid- to late-1800s, combining two popular sports: soccer and rugby. The sport at its origin looked much different than what fans enjoy today. Players' equipment was much less protective, the number of players on the sidelines was fewer, all playing fields were grass, and the size of the field was larger. Since rules were evolving in this new sport, quarterbacks had less ability to use the forward pass or take advantage of downfield blocking. Even the scoring system was different than it is now.

However, one significant fact has remained constant from the beginning: Success in American football requires reaching the "end zone." The game has always been a sort of chess match between a staff of coaches maneuvering players on both sides of the ball, and success requires strategy, strength of will, foresight, and talent. A defensive line of players exercises diligence to prevent an offensive side from crossing into the end zone. Offensive players create a variety of plays to work the length of the playing field strategically and skillfully, outsmarting the defense, to cross into the end zone.

Walter Camp has been hailed the "father of football," at least as we know American football today. Camp was said to have revolutionized the game with the introduction of "scrimmage rules." However, each team utilized these rules differently to take advantage of player talent and control the pace of the game. On one hand, a coach might use these rules to slow the pace of the game allowing the team to win with only one score. On the other hand, a coach might take advantage of the rules to increase the speed of the game with aggressive passing, thus forcing multiple scores to win. The more creative and innovative coaches became with their play-calling, the more challenging it became for the direction and adaptation of teams, along with creating improved scouting techniques for advanced preparation to win.

As technology, talent, and team dynamics have developed, the game of football has entered an entirely different realm from which it originated, but the goal is the same. Each team's understanding of winning, achievement, and success is all wrapped up in a nice little bow called the end zone. That 30-foot-long and 160-foot-wide space of turf represents the purpose for each coach, player, parent, and fan. It is all about getting to the end zone.

The same is true in leadership. Preparing to transition out of the Comfort Zone and leading through the Combat Zone ultimately have the same purpose: getting to the End Zone. What does the End Zone look like for you? How will you know you've reached the End Zone? Once you cross into the End Zone, what comes next? What steps are needed to help prevent recycling the organization through the Comfort Zone and facing the same challenges you overcame to reach the End Zone? The answers rest in understanding the characteristics of the End Zone and using the right tactical tools to lead wisely.

What is the End Zone?

The End Zone is not a destination but an opportunity to launch your ultimate desires for success. Once you recover from the battles of the Combat Zone, here is where you celebrate, but only briefly. On one hand, reaching the End Zone represents the completion of implementing the hard work required to lead through the most challenging and difficult times in your leadership. On the other hand, it is the opportunity to recover, evaluate, stretch, and perfect your leadership and the entire organization as you prepare for future growth.

You must resist the temptation of allowing the End Zone to become the new Comfort Zone. When you reach the End Zone, the success achieved can form a mindset that says, "If we keep our current processes in place, we will continue to grow." However, thinking such lays the foundation for the characteristics that initially placed you in the Comfort Zone. Once you understand the journey to the End Zone and what it provides when you arrive, you have a foundation to guide you through the conflict that accompanies changes required for future growth. What do each of the characteristics of the End Zone look like? It starts with recovering from the battles of the Combat Zone.

Recovery

Recovery is exactly what it sounds like: It is a time to rest, heal, and form new direction. After every football game, players usually take time to stretch, sit in an ice bath, get a massage, and rest, because they know there are more games to play. To be prepared for those games, they must recover from hard hits, strained or bruised muscles, and injuries incurred during the game. They also take time to examine what they learned during the game about themselves, their opponent, and areas they can improve upon to prepare for the next game. They reflect on the game plan they followed, mistakes they made, and great plays. Then, based on scouting reports, they develop a strategy for the next game. Players scrutinize their opponent's every move. They watch highlight reels for little changes or nuances that help them form a plan for the best approach to overcoming the opposing team. The process of recovery paves the way for future success.

I've learned that the same is true after the battles fought in the Combat Zone. The value of recovery is worth every minute given to it. As I mentioned in Chapter 2, combat can result in casualties. There are profits and losses, successes and failures, and areas of growth and decline. It leaves you and the organization with hard hits, strains, bruises, possible injuries, and at times, loss. However, once you have moved through conflict, the End Zone provides you a place to reflect on and work to heal each component of your leadership and the organization while forming direction for the future. A friend of mine in the business world refers to the overall process as "Post-Mortem." The purpose of post-mortem is to evaluate what did and did not work with the intent of making changes that will improve forward progress. The military refers to this as the "debrief." Colonel Dorminey was clear, "The mission isn't complete until it is debriefed. It is an integral part of the mission, not an afterthought. Regardless of if the mission was successful or not, there is always much to learn. Errors can be in planning (preparation) or in execution and often include communication errors."

Like a football player in recovery after a hard-fought game, leaders and organizations must recover after hard-fought conflicts in the Combat Zone. And ultimately, they must prepare to go another round. After rest, every member of the team or organization will appreciate the opportunity to heal and form new direction. Recovery allows both. Consider what this recovery process looks like for any organization and how you can create an environment of recovery when you reach the End Zone.

> *Every member of the team or organization will appreciate the opportunity to rest, heal, and form. Recovery allows all three.*

127

Healing

As you rest, recovery involves healing. Organizations need time to heal after working through the resistance brought on by conflict, addressing the fears created, and resolving the issues of trust. One step that is foundational to healing involves focusing on the positive changes made and your vision for the future. Healing will not occur as long as the remnants of negativity continue to surface. The discouragement created by negative emotions is detrimental to the progress of any organization. Highlight the positive changes that were made and how these changes lay the groundwork for success.

As I discussed in the previous chapter, you must focus on the vision. PK Benard once said, "A man without a vision is a man without a future, and a man without a future will always return to his past."[56] Take out the word "man" and insert your name or the name of your organization. To recover, organizations must focus on the vision. Their vision becomes the driving force behind every decision and action taken to move from where you are to where you want to go.

As a leader, how do you create an environment that is conducive for healing during recovery? Think about how you can implement one or more of these ideas.

Acknowledge. Do not shy away from acknowledging the negative impact of the Combat Zone or the Danger Zone. However, do not allow it to be the focus. Address it, and give others a chance to address it, then take time to heal.

Reflect. Take a moment to reflect on the previous weeks, months, or years. Introspection provides greater clarity to the progress made during this time. Encouraging others to reflect on their own personal growth will help them heal.

Process. One of the most powerful steps for me after reflecting on struggles from the Combat Zone is taking time to process. Everyone needs time to process what happened and what was learned. Keeping a journal of your thoughts as you process your experience will promote healing.

Listen. People want to know they are heard. What they have to say may not change the direction of the organization, but providing the space to express those feelings and genuinely listening to their concerns is a powerful gesture.

Assess. A healing environment requires an opportunity to assess the collateral damage. What losses were incurred? How did this affect each person? With assessment comes a consideration of everyone's needs in the organization.

Support. Organizations need a support structure in place that provides mental, emotional, physical, and even spiritual help. Supporting each person strengthens the overall health of the entire organization holistically.

Act. When people are confused about what can and cannot be done, leaders have an opportunity to act with empathy, compassion, understanding, and confidence. Your example speaks volumes in leading the actions of others. This is where the next success really starts.

Once you establish a pattern that you care about those who follow, you build trust, and progress improves. If other steps work for you and your organization, then use them. Each leader and organization must learn the most effective ways. Recovery establishes positive direction for your future and prevents resentment from bubbling. The recovery associated with healing is also directly tied to a forward direction.

Forming

Recovery not only affords us time for rest and healing, but it also provides opportunity for forming next steps. As we heal from the battles fought in the Combat Zone or Danger Zone, there is a need to be aware of what comes next. The battles do not end once we reach the End Zone. Celebrate and enjoy what has been achieved, but know there are more battles to fight to prevent the organization from developing a new level of complacency.

Forming direction for the future requires you to determine how to prepare for greater success. In the forming stage, you must focus your attention on a few key areas to ensure everyone remains fresh, physically equipped, mentally sharp, and excited about possibilities for new opportunities to grow. During this time, forming takes the shape of seven critical steps.

Research needed resources. Now is the best time to research available resources. How much gas do you have left in the tank? How much does your team have left? This step will help you determine how long the healing process will take. Additionally, the time you spend doing research to explore the resources needed for the future will assist you in determining both the capital, space, and workforce required to move forward with boldness.

Identify potential obstacles. New obstacles have a way of popping up at the most unexpected times. While you want to celebrate achievement, take time to reflect on the information gathered from your research and previous challenges. You also want to consider how the road ahead will present new obstacles and what they potentially look like.

Create a plan to address the obstacles. Working with a good team is one of the sweetest joys in any organization. Brainstorm with your team to identify these potential obstacles and what is needed to get ready. The insight of everyone who has suffered through the battles to get where you are will provide freshness to what was learned and how to be ready for the next battle.

Equip each member of the team. New challenges require new training. Proactive, ongoing training of each member of the team further strengthens the overall development of the organization. The more equipped each member becomes, the more potential you have for greater success.

Revisit your vision. I'm often asked, "How long should you develop a vision for?" My response is always, "It depends." I suggest revisiting the vision often. Your vision is directly connected to the needs of the organization, and as those needs change, so does the vision. Take time to consider where you are in reaching the vision and if you need to adjust.

Set new goals. Goals are essential to the success of any organization. The type of goals you establish directly impacts the motivation and team effort to achieve them. You achieved goals to reach the End Zone. Do not rest long! Now is the time to do your strategic planning. Ensure goals are challenging, energizing, and meaningful to everyone involved.

Adjust accordingly. Your ability as a leader to adjust rounds out a healthy list for forming new direction. Adjusting does not diminish the success of the organization. It demonstrates your leadership to research needed resources, identify obstacles, create a plan, equip each member of the team, focus on the vision, and set new goals.

During and after the recovery phase, you have time to reflect on where you've been, what you experienced, what you learned from those experiences, along with how and when you want to move forward with this new information. Learning about your abilities to lead is critical for improving your leadership in the future. During this time, you have opportunity to think more deeply about how your failures and successes have affected your leadership and organization. Based on what you learn, you can sustain or make necessary corrections.

Reaching the End Zone is far more than just a time of celebration. You will celebrate, but the End Zone makes it possible for you to recover. You will rest, heal, and form direction for the future. The result makes you stronger as a leader and as an organization. Use this opportunity to watch how you and the team flourish.

Real Success

Any time the word "real" is attached as a descriptor, there is an implication that something else is not real—or, in other words, it is false. Time and time again, people fall into the trap of believing in a false sense of success. Why is it that every generation struggles with this same failure? Perhaps, as I have already mentioned, it is because we have mis-defined success by relying on markers that do not characterize true victory. Let me discuss a few examples.

Money

One of the most exhausted measures of success is money. Someone's value or worth is often associated with the size of their bank account. More than one individual has risked life and limb, sacrificed friend, family, and foe, or forfeited rest and recreation, all to achieve success as defined by wealth. What drives people to such extremes in the pursuit of money? While it is easy to dismiss such behavior as silly and unwise, I believe it often starts innocently.

Survival requires you to obtain some level of wealth. Parents desire to provide their children with more than what they had growing up to whatever degree they believe is helpful. They may work overtime, or pick up a part-time job, to have money for the extra-curricular activities their children enjoy. But like a snowball tumbling down a hill, the blinded pursuit of wealth can turn our best intentions into ugly behavior. Once the snowball has been tightly packed and begins its descent, it gathers more snow with each revolution and grows to frightening proportions, threatening destruction to everyone or everything in its path. When it comes to wealth accumulation, the initial intentions are often pure, but those intentions can quickly devolve into greed, and people lack the self-reflection required to see this snowball effect happening and stop its progress. The truth is evident in the overwhelming amount of revolving debt average Americans have amassed. According to an article in USA Today, on average Americans hold four credit cards with over $6,000 debt on each.[57] The math is staggering. More than a trillion dollars in revolving debt plagues Americans, and the reasons are complex. Between mortgage or rent payments, two or more auto payments, and credit card debt, Americans have not succeeded in living within their means. The consequence comes at a high price. Sadly, with the increase in the cost of food and fuel, a change does not seem to be forthcoming any time soon.

Perhaps a bit harsher reason is born out of greed. Most Americans would agree that capitalism has powerful benefits, but it also has strong consequences. It lends itself toward the unhealthy nature of greed. At the heart of capitalism is the private ownership of business motivated by the profit margin.

After all, no one enters business with the purpose of losing money. However, making a profit is not the problem. The problem enters when the motivation for profit becomes so consuming that individuals, teams, and organizations compromise their core values to accumulate more. When greed is imbedded in your heart as a leader, your pursuit of financial

> *When greed is embedded in your heart as a leader, your pursuit of financial achievement stops at nothing short of "whatever it takes."*

achievement stops at nothing short of "whatever it takes." The moral and ethical compass points only in the direction of self-advancement. The core values established by teamwork, organizational integrity, or personal reputation all take a back seat to greater wealth and prosperity. And when you finally gain that wealth or hit that target profit margin, it is never enough to quench your thirst. This relentless pursuit idolizes money as a (false) marker of success.

Possessions

The pursuit of possessions is directly associated with the pursuit of money. While some measure success by how much money they have in the bank, others measure it by the number of possessions they accumulate. This may manifest in the form of land, houses, cars, jewelry, musical instruments, antiques, rare collectible items, or hundreds of other things. "Things" is the key word here. These material possessions are simply things used to measure success.

The obsession with possessions drives people to spend whatever amount of time and money is needed to obtain them. The rarer the item, the more effort put forth to get it. I understand the investment value of certain items of this nature. Investing for future retirement or for hobbies is not what I'm discussing here. But for someone who measures their success based on the material possessions they accumulate, the intent is not to secure a retirement fund or invest in the future. The intent is simply to *have*.

I've known plenty of people who have spent their lives amassing possessions. As with those who pursue money, these individuals dedicate their life to obtaining as many rare gems as possible at the sacrifice of time with family and their own physical health. And as with those who pursue money, these individuals often spend their lives trying to fill a void that never gets filled. Money and possessions can be fine in moderation, and every person has a choice of how to spend their lives. But, like the adage says, "I've never seen a hearse pulling a U-Haul trailer." You can't take it with you when you go.

Prestige

Another area that is often used to define or characterize success is the level of prestige one achieves. One can seek prestige in education, title, retirement, tenure, or award. Achievement in any of these areas is not wrong, just like there is nothing wrong with money and possessions. But defining success by prestige can cause dissatisfaction. Oftentimes, what looks best on paper is not what actually satisfies your soul or brings you happiness. And striving for prestigious accolades that aren't right for you can distract you from your true purpose.

The problem with chasing prestige is that it is always focused on what *others* think—the concept centers on defining yourself according to someone else's standard. Furthermore, one can easily use prestige as a shortcut in defining goals, which can cause them to be less intentional about what kind of leader they want to be and where they want their organization to go. This lack of introspection and intentionality can lead right back to the Comfort Zone or the Danger Zone. Ultimately, if you willingly sacrifice health and family to achieve a level of education, a job title, or a tenure for retirement, you may find yourself regretting the long-term effects.

Whether it's money, possessions, or prestige, leaders need to be aware of how they measure success and what they are willing to do to reach that level of success. Life is too short to sacrifice your family and health for something like money, material possessions, or a level of prestige that will not last. How can the pitfalls mentioned be avoided?

Self-evaluation. Self-evaluation is a great place to start. I mentioned priorities as a strategy to lead through the Combat Zone and the Danger Zone. But they are also relevant to the work you do in the End Zone. Defining priorities, however, can be as tricky as defining real success. Each person establishes priorities based on several factors, such as survival, family, health, finance, better relationships, and self-improvement. Within each category, a variety of levels exist, complicating priorities further. I've heard people say that if you want to know someone's priorities, look at their bank statement. This may or may not be an accurate assessment of priorities, but I can safely say that when you sit down and examine where and how you spend your money, a solid picture emerges about what you prioritize.

Contentment. One practice that can correct the self-destructive path of the financial rush is to learn and value contentment. This idea has been reverberated in a number of ways. Benjamin Franklin once said, "Content makes poor men rich. Discontent makes rich men poor." Socrates said, "He is richest who is content with the least, for content is the wealth of nature." Would you agree? Perhaps the best way to understand the value of contentment is to examine the effects of discontent. For example, it is said that when John D. Rockefeller was asked, "How much money is enough?", he responded, "Just a little bit more." Far too often, the insatiable desire for more

> *All the wealth the world has to offer means nothing if you lose everything of value to have it.*

requires you to sacrifice peace, hope, and integrity on the altar of your heart and soul. Until you realize that the concept of enough is more about your attitude than the amount you have, you will never learn the needed contentment to attain real success. All the wealth the world has to offer means nothing if you lose everything of value to have it.

Time management. Another measure of your priorities is found in how you spend your time. Frighteningly, your smart devices keep a log of how much time you spend on your screens. If set up, once a week, the device will notify you of your average time per day with the screen open. Most users have no idea how quickly they rack up hours staring at a device. If someone told you that, on average, you spend thirty-five hours a week looking at your phone, would you be shocked? What does that say about your priorities?

As a leader, you're responsible for the monumental task of influencing people to move from point A to point B to achieve a measure of success. The momentum built during this process is essential to helping individuals, teams, and organizations lift themselves out of any rut or stalemate and step into the future. Rather than focusing on money, possessions, or prestige, you can achieve real success by focusing on two areas: relationships and the realization of hope.

Relationships

What gives meaning to life? You need a specific mental image that, when visualized and accomplished, gives fulfillment. At the end of life, everyone wants to know that what they accomplished in life was meaningful. While each person may interpret the term *meaningful* a bit differently, for you to live a fulfilled life, you know it must be meaningful.

I believe we would all agree that the close relationships formed with family provide a great deal of meaning. We also understand the value of relationships developed between friends. The term we often use to describe it is "best friends." I would be remiss to not mention the relationships between neighbors, coworkers, and citizens of the community. The closer your relationships become, the more meaningful you see them.

As a leader, you learn more each day about the value of relationships and the importance of helping others reach their potential. I grew up hearing leaders talk about "working themselves out of a job." On the surface, the idea seemed like a paradox. After all, if a person needs a job, why would they work themselves out of it? As I matured, however, I began to realize the significance of this thought.

In his *Forbes* article, "Make Yourself Dispensable," Jack Reichert claims, "Your value to your company should not be, in fact, that you are the crucial piece that keeps everything running; rather, your value to your company should be that without you the company might run fine, but it wouldn't excel."[58] His approach to becoming dispensable identifies three steps, two of which involve surrounding yourself with people who threaten your job along with those who have an ability to set things up to run without you. You make yourself dispensable through creating an environment where others reach their greatest potential and success. The greatest legacy you can leave to any organization

> *The greatest legacy you can leave to any organization is the ability for others to successfully continue to do great things without you.*

is the ability for others to successfully continue to do great things without you. In the overall scope of an organization, the people who can do so are truly indispensable. Relationships built around this concept contribute to a meaningful life. How you build this legacy, or succession plan, is based on five key ideas.

Invitation. Start by inviting a few who are willing to prepare themselves for leadership. One of your roles as a leader is to recognize the abilities of those who follow. Before you recognize someone's educational level, notice those with courage and character, people who work for the good of others and voice concerns over injustices, and invite them into a role where they can further develop these incredible attributes.

Investment. The greater the investment, the greater the return. The bottom line here is about sharing life together. Life is a journey, and the amount of time it takes for your investment to produce a return will depend on the individual. Do not enter the relationship with a time frame in mind. Rather, use the time as an opportunity to get to know these future leaders. More importantly, use it as an opportunity for them to know you. They need to know you are real, to learn about your challenges and struggles, and to understand what gets you up each morning and drives you as a leader. As the relationship grows, your example as a leader will become a guiding force in their lives, one they will rely on long after you are gone.

Instruction. The future of leadership in any organization requires you to instruct these future leaders in everything they need to know about leading. Empathy, emotional intelligence, conflict resolution, decision-making, communication, etc. are specific components of leadership you can model and teach. The time you invest in developing your relationship with these future leaders is one piece of your legacy. What I'm referring to here involves a more formal sit-down opportunity to give instruction in the qualities and characteristics needed to develop them into a great leader.

Inclusion. At a workshop in Dallas, an Army officer discussed three important terms with me: diversity, inclusion, and belonging. Her definition of each was insightful. "Diversity means we all have a seat at the table. Inclusion means everyone has a voice at the table. Belonging means every voice is heard." Inclusion means more than just giving everyone a voice. Instead of attempting to identify the "Who's Who" at the leadership academy, look at every person as a potential leader in your organization. Some of the greatest leaders were not the best academic candidates. Once included, if you want to create a legacy to last generations, learn to involve these future leaders in a leadership role and listen to them. When you do, they will grow and learn to do the same.

Intentionality. Your legacy will not happen by accident. You must intentionally structure the direction of any future leader in two areas: growth and reproduction. First, they must grow into their leadership. All great leaders are learning leaders. Create this learning heart in each of those who follow your legacy. Second, it must not end with them. Encourage these future leaders to think about who they can influence and work with to prepare as a leader that will replace them. Again, this type of legacy does not happen by accident. You must intentionally focus their attention on growth and reproduction.

Succession plans and templates are generally unique to each organization. However, there is a plethora of books and articles on the subject. The concepts are crafted to provide direction for your leadership. I've found that these five basic ideas provide the positive foundation. If you develop relationships that prepare others to succeed without you, your legacy will survive for generations.

Realization of Hope

Too often the word hope is used with an element of doubt. It is more like a wish, with a level of uncertainty. You may really want something to happen, but you are unsure if it will. For example, your favorite sports team is scheduled for a playoff game, and you *hope* they win but you know there is a possibility they will not. When it comes to the weather, you may *hope* for sunshine or rain but, again, you cannot always rely on the meteorologist.

You will also find that some people live with a false sense of hope. This type of hope is based on false expectations or inaccurate and even intentionally false information. When your hope stems from these sources, you may feel hopeful, but your hope is empty, because the foundation is weak. The damage can be irreparable.

Worse than a false sense of hope is living without hope. Far too many people in the world today live without any hope. They have no hope for a brighter and more successful future. One example of hopelessness many can relate to occurs when suffering loss, perhaps the loss of a loved one. You can also live without hope when you lose a job, receive a terminal diagnosis, encounter an unexpected tragedy, or simply receive bad news. Watching the news media today can provide many opportunities for one to adopt a state of hopelessness, as you are bombarded with stories about war, famine, abuse, the spread of the pandemic, and so much more. During these situations, it is more critical than ever to realize there is hope.

The realization of hope goes far beyond a wish. Wishes are dreams without goals and plans. A wish lacks a level of expectation. Genuine hope takes you beyond your wishes and dreams. By contrast, hope involves an earnest expectation. It is desire plus expectation. You not only desire to receive something, but you expect to receive it. The only way this kind of hope exists is when you prepare for it. Hope is not by chance or accidental. You don't just hope, and then something happens. You lay the right foundation. At this point, your realization of hope justifies expectation.

Real success can never be measured in terms of money, material possessions, or prestige. Real success is built around the deep and meaningful relationships developed in leading others to their greatest potential. Further, the realization of hope combines your desires with an expectation, and when your hope lives, your leadership thrives. When these two components come together, you begin to enjoy real success.

Celebrating Achievement

When a football player scores a touchdown, fans and nonfans alike witness a celebration as the player performs various dance moves, spikes the football, jumps up and shares his excitement with a devoted fan, or chest-bumps fellow players. There is no mistaking their excitement as the scoring team crosses the goal line. The entire team, along with staff, coaches, and fans all join in the celebration. Although the celebration is short-lived, that brief moment is time to enjoy a victory. Even when teams are behind and have no potential to win the game, they celebrate when they score a touchdown.

The End Zone represents achievement. It is a time to celebrate. After the casualties, hard hits, bruises, and injuries suffered in the Combat Zone, everyone is ready to celebrate, and you need to provide it. Celebrate along the way because every step invites you to acknowledge growth. But, when you finally cross the finish line, having carried out the plans and achieved every goal, every member of the organization deserves to enjoy the success. This time of celebration is an opportunity to build more rapport with your team by taking a moment to acknowledge their contributions and thank them.

Every organization celebrates achievement differently. Not all celebration requires financial compensation. Not all celebration involves something big. However, celebrating achievement does promote future growth and success. Let me share two key suggestions.

Acknowledge the achievement

A simple word of encouragement carries more weight than I can express. Affirming an individual's work or a team's contribution secures the continuation of their efforts. Develop the practice of sending a card, an email, text, or better yet, talk to them face-to-face and share your appreciation for the achievement. Be specific. Tell others.

When people in the organization learn that you acknowledge their achievement, it will accomplish at least one of three things: One, it creates a greater sense of value. People want to know their work is valued and appreciated. Two, it will strengthen the loyalty of the individual or team. Once people know you value their work, they have a stronger desire to do more for you. Three, it will motivate others in the organization to step up and do more. Word spreads quickly in an organization. When people see their colleagues and coworkers acknowledged for their contribution, it raises the bar for others to participate in the same.

The power of words cannot be overstated. Your ability to recognize and acknowledge achievement strengthens your leadership, and it increases the desire of others to follow.

Determine how you can provide encouragement and watch how it changes the people you lead.

Award the achievement

Awards fall into several categories from food (dinner out) to finances (bonus or raise) to time off (vacation), and the list goes on. The best way to know what produces the greatest impact is to learn people's self-interests. What motivates everyone in your organization? Once you know the answer to this question, you can tailor the awards specifically.

Awarding achievement with financial compensation remains one of the strongest motivators for production. A bonus or raise does not always require large amounts of money to express appreciation. However, when a larger bonus or raise is feasible, an individual feels a greater sense of value. I realize there are times when a bonus or raise is not possible. When this is the case, remember that time away from the job can be just as valuable and motivating. Few areas speak to self-interests like paid time off, whether a vacation or a staycation.

You can create competition with recognition awards for various levels of work. These can be presented at a special awards ceremony or event: most sales, best attitude, customer service, outstanding leadership, overachiever, servant, character, teamwork, etc. *Healthy* competition produces greater achievement, even when people know they are vying for such an award. *Unhealthy* competition can destroy all you work to achieve and become a cancer that eats away at the organization. You need to be aware of the differences for your leadership and team. Then, use what builds a more exciting workplace.

You must exercise caution to avoid the opposite. Col. Dorminey warned leaders of this danger. "One pitfall I've seen is rewarding the lack of achievement…everyone gets a trophy. This undermines the credibility of the leader and becomes a demotivator to those that really deserve the recognition. Taking care of your people includes awarding achievement as much as it does holding lack luster performers accountable."

These celebratory moments are designed to build momentum. The enthusiasm becomes contagious as every member of the team recognizes what the organization has accomplished. The celebration allows every member of the team to feel valued. As momentum builds, each achievement toward the future creates greater excitement. As Andy Stanley once wrote, "What gets celebrated, gets repeated."[59] Do not underestimate the power of building momentum through celebrating achievement. Everyone in the organization will appreciate the recognition.

Evaluation

Two types of evaluation fuel leaders toward progress in the End Zone: formative and summative. Leaders need the first to guide them through each Zone and the second assists them as they push forward to greater success. Formative evaluation is a more fundamental approach that involves continually evaluating the process along the way. With each benchmark, leaders evaluate progress. This includes an evaluation before designing the plan and an evaluation of progress throughout the execution of the plan. Adjustments can be made during these evaluative sessions based on how progress measures up to expectations.

Summative evaluation occurs when the entire project or work has been completed. You review the entire project of work, evaluating what worked, what did not, and what was learned. This evaluation will enable you to further determine what modifications can be made to improve direction and progress for the future of the organization. Summative evaluation is primarily connected to the End Zone because, once you have celebrated achievement, it is time to consider how you will move ahead to future success.

You will face the challenge of how to address failure. What didn't work and why? While it is uncertain who first said it, the thought is still powerful, "Failure is not fatal, and success is not final." When evaluating failure, you must not allow falling short of goals to force hasty decisions that can further impact forward progress in your leadership or the organization. At the same time, success must not be allowed to create an attitude of pride, which can have the same result. How do you deal with failure when it comes.

Managing failure

Evaluating your journey to the End Zone will point to areas of weakness and, at times, places where you encountered failure. Like success, failure is an attitude. Defining failure ranges from not getting what you want to total bankruptcy. The way someone defines failure hinges on how they define success. If success is based on money, possessions, or prestige, then failure occurs when you fall short of receiving or achieving the standard you set for them. If success is based on relationships or the realization of hope, then failure looks completely different because it is based on a qualitative measurement you assign to those areas. Failure may surface in the form of broken relationships or the loss of hope. Your perspective will determine the long-term impact failure has on your leadership and organization. How can you manage times when failure happens?

Welcome failure. Everyone experiences failure. Without it, success is not nearly as sweet. It may seem counterintuitive, but failure can strengthen your ability to lead during the most difficult times in life. Think like a champion.

Tom Hopkins suggests that failure should be seen through the eyes of a champion.[60] When champions fail, their attitude is one that sees failure as opportunity, an opportunity to change direction, develop a sense of humor, practice technique, and perfect performance. Welcoming failure is a foundational attitude for coping with or managing it.

Learn from failure. *Some of the greatest opportunities in life are associated with failure.* The primary reason is because failure reveals how *not* to do something. When it came to the invention of the light bulb, it is commonly known that Thomas Edison claimed, "I have not failed. I have just found 10,000 ways that won't work." What you learn from the ways you or your organization fall short, it impacts your view of failure. Evaluation allows you to focus on what is and what is not working well. When failure exists, learn from what didn't work and make corrections.

Distinguish *what* from *who*. No matter what happens, know that *you* are not a failure, you just had a setback. *What* you implement may not have worked, but that does not characterize *who* you are as a leader. Distinguish these two concepts. Based on what you learn from failing, the next program you implement may be the catalyst for great success. You will experience setbacks that impact you and the entire organization. However, there is a difference between your activity and your identity.

Own it. Ownership plays a key role in failure. Examine your responsibility and do not be afraid to own up to the mistakes that were made. Acknowledging your responsibilities and owning it builds credibility among team members. One of the most powerful thoughts I've learned as a leader is that when you win, give credit to the team. When you fail, take responsibility as the leader. Casting blame on someone or something else does not promote good leadership and it weakens team morale.

Move on. Failure only occurs when you allow the setback to hinder your forward progress, or you give up completely. *Do not allow failure to linger.* The more obsessed you become with an area that did not work as planned, the more likely you are to slow or stop forward progress. Learn from it and take steps to move ahead. This is why evaluation is so important. Let the failures encountered provide needed motivation for you and your team to take steps that stretch and perfect your leadership.

Evaluation should be viewed as what I call a "recycling opportunity." A recycling opportunity gives you a chance to sift through every area of success and failure within previous quarters and determine what can be used again and built upon to provide a more solid foundation for future work, or what needs to be avoided. Recycling specific ideas, plans, projects, and people skills can build morale among team members, breathe life into new goals, and add value to how an organization builds greater success.

Stretching Yourself

Few things are more exciting for leaders than the opportunity to grow. Upon leaving the Comfort Zone and battling through the Combat Zone, the End Zone opens doors for growth. In her book, *GRIT: The Power of Passion and Perseverance*, Angela Duckworth learned that people who are the most successful in their fields focus on a specific area—usually not one of strength but of weakness—and they intentionally find whatever is needed to challenge them, what she refers to as "stretch goals."[61] The deliberate nature of this practice makes it possible to improve, turning weakness into strength. The design of these stretch goals is to direct your attention and practice in areas you don't do well to improve them.

You will find it beneficial to realize early on that you cannot remain in the same place. No organization grows standing still. If you continue traveling the same course without making necessary adjustments, you will experience stagnation at best and a decline with the potential of closure at worse. Change is an essential requirement for growth. What do you need to know and do to stretch yourself? Consider a few suggestions.

> *Change is an essential requirement to growth.*

Know your weaknesses. If you want to stretch yourself as a leader, it is essential to know specific areas that need work. Only then can you spend the appropriate time honing those skills in your leadership. When you can identify areas of vulnerability and expose shortcomings you can develop a plan that stretches you in ways to direct behavioral change.

Invite input. Find a mentor who can help evaluate your leadership and suggest ways to push you further to grow. If you cannot find a mentor, invite outside resources to examine the influence of your leadership and assist you in strengthening your ability to lead.

Look to the latest trends. Pay attention to changes in the culture surrounding the organization and recipients of your product or service. What do these trends tell you? Are there changes you need to make to improve your product or service? The power of observation is immeasurable. Asking a few questions and a willingness to adjust ensures progress.

Grow your leadership. Continuing education is essential. Take a course, attend a workshop, or read the most current books. Do something to improve your abilities. Encourage everyone in your organization to participate in personal growth and development. The more educated and informed they are, the stronger the organization becomes and the better your leadership.

Build your teams. Invite field specialists into your organization to identify gaps and find ways to help your team become more cohesive. An unbiased perspective and guidance are excellent ways to identify areas where changes can be made to improve synergy. A third-party review also provides another opportunity to identify and celebrate processes and relationships that promote growth and increase productivity. Building a team is not always about getting the best from each field. You may find top talent in every area, but if they cannot work together, you will not succeed. Focus on building cohesiveness. Less talented teams that work well together will outperform teams with great talent that do not. Teams must support and strengthen one another in working together, not fighting to be better than others on the team.

Remain vigilant. Be aware that the success enjoyed in the End Zone can become the next Comfort Zone for you if you do not focus on stretching yourself further. It's easy to be lulled into complacency when you do not remain vigilant because the tendency is to create a new level of comfort. You must persevere.

Additional measures depend on the individual culture and specific needs of your leadership and organization. The time spent to stretch yourself as a leader is an investment that pays strong dividends in the success of any organization. The law of the harvest holds true for you and your leadership as it does in every area of life: The more seed you sow, the greater the harvest.

Perfecting Leadership

Much like stretching yourself, perfecting your leadership is a natural result of reaching the End Zone. With this section, however, I want to focus more on areas related to eliminating the weaker sides of your leadership and strengthening the others. To accomplish this task, you must be willing to take the time for self-evaluation, or as I mentioned earlier, *introspection*. Looking inward to discover what you know about yourself, but are not always willing to admit, takes courage and a desire to improve.

GiANT is an organization designed to accomplish this purpose. The various training tools available to every leader focus on the best ways to perfect your leadership and the leadership abilities of everyone around you. In Chapter 1, I referenced a book by Jeremie Kubicek and Steve Cockram called *100x Leader*. In this book, they describe a group of guides responsible for leading people to the top of Mount Everest and back down safely. These guides are known as Sherpa. One of the thoughts that resonated most with me was the fact that Sherpa do not count how many times they have been up the mountain, but rather how many people they have taken up the mountain. If you know anything about Mount Everest, you know the incredible danger involved and the demands on one's physical body to accomplish such a

> *You perfect your leadership, not by focusing on reaching your own potential, but by how many others you elevate to reach their potential as a leader.*

feat. The beauty of the mindset possessed by these guides is a great lesson for you as a leader. You perfect your leadership, not by focusing on reaching your own potential, but by how many others you elevate to reach their potential as a leader.

Perfecting your leadership may be subjective to your context and leadership style. My son-in-law reminded me that the quest towards perfect leadership is unending, and we must be unyielding. Four basic components will assist you down this path.

Discipline. Discipline is a staple for every leader. The mental fortitude you develop with discipline will directly influence your ability to perfect your leadership. The mastery of any leadership skill, quality, or style is based on discipline. My first leadership role involved managing a commercial construction rental company. I will never forget the owner's words to me when I began, "If it were easy, everyone would do it." He wanted me to know it would take discipline to enjoy success as a leader, and not everyone was willing to take the more difficult path to achieve it. To lead means to be disciplined. Be disciplined in every area of your life, whether at home or work.

Balance. Leadership requires balance. I am frequently asked, "How do you balance the relationship between work and home?" The perpetual tug of war we play while seeking work-life balance is exhausting. Few areas are more challenging or relevant but finding and maintaining an appropriate work-life balance will allow you to be more effective in all areas of your life. By establishing healthy boundaries, you provide yourself more opportunities to better focus your efforts. I prefer to think of this concept as work-life *value*. What you value most will become your focus. If you find value in your job (title, position, or project), then you talk about it, spend more time in it, and focus your life on it. However, if you find value at home (husband/father, wife/mother, etc.), then you will focus your time, attention, and conversation improving it. This does not mean work is invaluable. It does mean you need to evaluate how you will handle the situation. Let me share three possibilities: First, know your core values, write them down, and review them every day. Second, determine your limits. As I have already discussed, it is important to manage your time well, and learn the value of when to say yes and no. Be careful not to overextend yourself. Third, remember you are a leader in both your home and the office. Take the same responsibility and give the same effort to leading at home, if not more, as you do at work. Your success at home will directly impact your success at work. The reverse is not always true.

Passion. I wish I could make every leader passionate about leading. As you know, it does not work this way. Passion is essential to you as a leader. While the idea of passion often reflects excitement and enthusiasm, the origin of this word is based in suffering and sacrifice. Discovering or developing passion is directly connected to your level of perseverance. We tend to persevere in areas we are most passionate about. I was encouraged to ask myself three questions, and I urge you to do the same: 1) What do you really want? 2) Why do you want it? 3) How badly do you want it? Then write out what you are *willing* to give up for it and what you are *not willing* to give up. Your responses will help you identify what you are passionate about and lay the groundwork for how you can successfully reach the goals you are most passionate about. Once you know where your passion lies, pursue it with all your strength.

Practice. Perfecting your leadership is not about doing something one time, but many. A good friend once told me, "Practice does not make perfect, but *perfect* practice makes perfect." The implication of this thought is a reminder to focus on the weaknesses you need as strengths. This focus may involve developing an area of personal weakness or finding someone whose strength compliments your weakness. A friend of mine told me, "Hire to your weakness. Avoid the tendency to hire just like you. You have blind spots. Hire someone to help you cover them." This type of intentionality and practice brings us full circle. Practice requires a disciplined mindset. The time you designate to improving your leadership produces lasting influence in your family and organization. As a leader, remember the End Zone is not a destination, but an opportunity to continue working on your leadership abilities. The more you practice the better your leadership becomes.

Everyone loves reaching the End Zone. However, you must realize it does not represent the end. The End Zone signifies the beginning of something greater for the future. You recover (heal and form). You enjoy real success (relationships and the realization of hope). You celebrate your achievements (acknowledge and award). You evaluate. You stretch yourself further. And you perfect your leadership. The plans were implemented, and the goals achieved. However, you cannot rest too long for fear of inadvertently stumbling into a new Comfort Zone. Being aware of this fact will help you avoid drifting back into the Combat Zone, or worse, the Danger Zone.

Therefore, you must establish a way forward that builds on the current success with a design and intent for improving. What will help you continue to grow as a leader? How do you become an even stronger organization? How will you motivate your team to learn so they can continue to build momentum as they face new challenges? As I will unfold in the next chapter, you need a strategy—but not just any strategy. You need "7 Tactics for Leading in the Zones."

In The End Zone

1. Which characteristics in the End Zone do you see in your organization's current leadership?

   a. Recovery
   b. Real Success
   c. Celebrating Achievement
   d. Evaluation
   e. Stretching Yourself
   f. Perfecting Leadership

2. How does your organization define success? Does the definition align with the core values of the organization?

3. What steps do leaders in the organization take to promote greater achievement among all members of the team?

4. How is achievement communicated and celebrated throughout the organization?

5. Describe the path each member of the team is provided to stretch their abilities and grow the organization.

6. What changes could be made to help your organization promote greater leadership development from within?

Chapter Five

7 Tactics for Leading in the Zones

"Planning is bringing the future into the present so that you can do something about it now."
Alan Lakein

When I interviewed him, General Greg Chaney said, "No combat situation is a 'shoot from the hip' operation. Every operation or mission has some level of planning, and you want to maximize the length of time you have to plan." Successfully addressing change requires a strategy, but what does this type of strategy look like? I propose a strategy that consists of seven tactics. The purpose of these tactics is to provide you with essential tools that will equip you to lead and steps to carefully guide you through each Zone. They will also provide foundational concepts to aid you in applying the specific application discussed in previous chapters.

As I have mentioned, the only way to move out of your Comfort Zone is by introducing change. When change is introduced, conflict will soon follow, and when you encounter conflict, you must lead through the Combat Zone. During times of conflict, you must avoid returning to the familiar and predictable comfort of the past while carefully avoiding the Danger Zone. Leading through these turbulent times requires you to understand who you are and where you are headed. You need vision, a mission, and the ability to execute a strategy. As you read this chapter, consider a few questions.

What is your vision? As you look to the future, there must be an image of who you want to be, what you want your organization to look like. The vision drives everything, so make sure it is clearly communicated and easy to understand.

What is the mission? The purpose for which the organization exists must be clear before establishing and executing a strategy to achieve it. The mission is the engine to your vision. The operational goals set during the strategic planning process will allow the organization to monitor progress and determine what adjustments must be made to achieve the vision.

What are the greatest needs of the organization? Without understanding the needs of the organization, it is difficult to plan a proper strategy. Ultimately, the design of any strategy is to address these needs. Discuss the needs within each department of the organization and overall. List them and identify the threads you find.

Who will you serve? The organizational mission must involve serving others. The people who physically and mentally contribute to achieving the mission need to know that their work means something and that it will serve the greater good of others. How will the world be better when you accomplish the objective?

What are the strengths and weaknesses of the organization? Determining the strengths and weaknesses of any organization makes it possible to know what can and cannot be achieved. Once you understand these components, you have an opportunity to lay out the right steps within the strategy.

Given the strengths and weaknesses, what opportunities exist? When you have a grasp of both the strengths and weaknesses, you begin to explore opportunities. Based on your strengths, what do the possibilities look like? When you can see the possibilities, doors tend to open by which you can take advantage of the opportunities.

What threats exist? A key part of the SWOT analysis, identifying external characteristics or circumstances that are harmful to achieving your goals is an essential step. If threats and weaknesses are greater than the strengths and opportunities, modifications are required. When working toward achievement, knowing these threats will aid you as a leader.

Based on the strengths and opportunities of the organization, what do you desire to achieve? The desire to achieve success for any organization can only be built on strengths and opportunities. When clearly defined, these become building blocks to outline a positive direction for the future of the organization.

How and when will you evaluate progress? Establishing benchmarks will assist you in understanding the right time to adjust. These adjustments help determine the proper steps for your team to continually access operational objectives that confirm the organization has implemented the most effective approach to achieving the mission.

How will you reward each part of the organization when the strategy is accomplished? As I have stated, celebrating each successful step ensures a repetition of the components initiated to achieve it. Do not underestimate the importance of rewarding people for a job well done. Each time you celebrate, you strengthen your leadership and ensure the loyalty of each person committed to achieving the vision and mission of the organization.

To implement an effective strategy, you must dig deeply into all areas. A better understanding of what could hinder success will aid you in creating a comprehensive plan to guide your organization to the End Zone. The way you answer the questions above will determine how you move forward. How well you implement your strategy directly impacts your level of success. In my interview with Captain Torian, he referenced a tool developed by Air Force Colonel John Boyd called the OODA loop. This figure explains the basics of how the loop functions.

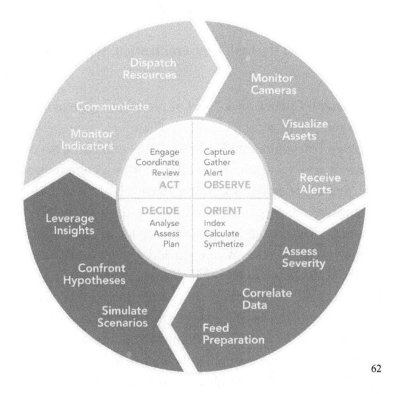

62

The iterative nature of the OODA loop strengthens the process for working through this strategy. As Brett and Kate McKay explained, "The OODA loop is an explicit representation of the process that human beings and organizations use to learn, grow, and thrive in a rapidly changing environment—be it in war, business, or life."[63] While Boyd developed a more complex diagram, when leaders learn to *observe* (gather new information about the environment or circumstances), *orient* (assess and calculate how to interact with a new environment), *decide* (analyze best ways to move forward), and *act* (implement or test the theory), they build a strong foundation for greater success. In addition to the principles, suggestions to follow, and pitfalls to avoid, as explained in previous chapters, these four concepts have influenced the discussion within each tactic of this chapter.

Tactic 1: ReCON: Rethink Communication, Operation, and Negotiation

General Chaney said, "Part of planning is to make sure you do some sort of reconnaissance." Therefore, in preparing any strategy you begin with ReCON, that is rethinking several key areas of your leadership, including how you communicate, operate, and negotiate. Before I dive into each of these three areas, consider the significance of how you think or, in this case, rethink. The cognitive battle you engage in as a leader will challenge you to the core. When you add the stress of leading others, the walls begin to feel as if they are closing in on you. It is time to rethink. What exactly do you need to rethink as a leader? How will this exercise make any difference to the current situation? Few tactics will impact the future of your leadership as much as developing the ability to effectively rethink your current position, which is critical to the success of your strategy. Lieutenant Colonel Lewis said it best: "You lead from the front. You can't lead from the rear." He went on to clarify that leaders are responsible for knowing what motivates their followers and then motivating them to do the task at hand. Rethinking your position increases your credibility and strengthens your ability to lead.

> *Self-evaluation motivates you to stretch your abilities in ways you never thought possible.*

Self-evaluation motivates you to stretch your abilities in ways you never thought possible. In part, you may need to rethink your leadership style, i.e., your approach to those you lead and how best to motivate them. Three of the most significant books on relationships for leaders were written by the Arbinger Institute: *Leadership and Self-Deception, The Anatomy of Peace,* and *The Outward Mindset.*[64] These three gems analyze what healthy relationships look like, emphasizing that your words, actions, and decisions impact others. The thought process involved provides a foundation for building healthy relationships. Will your words, actions, and decisions make the other person's life better, safer, and more successful? Will they reach their greatest potential because of your leadership? Are you thinking outwardly about the effect of your leadership? The moment you allow every word, action, and decision to be focused on yourself, you begin losing the battle and the consequences are often irreparable.

Communication

Even if you neglect rethinking your operations or negotiations, you must rethink your communication skills. Poor communication often dominates the home and workplace. General Chaney said, "The common denominator for communication is trust. You must have trust before you can have communication. You may hand out all the documents, use PowerPoint, and be the most dynamic speaker, but if people don't trust you or trust that what you are saying is accurate, they will not hear what you have to say."

Effective communication is priority one throughout the implementation of this strategy. The key word is *effective*, and by using this word, as it relates to communication, I am referring to the *means* we use to communicate. Let me clarify the significance of what I mean here in reference to communication.

If you are not careful, there can be a major disconnect between what you think you are saying and your actual words. An effective communicator doesn't simply hope that *what* the other person hears is what the one speaking *wanted* them to hear. Instead, they increase their awareness, so the audience hears the message correctly. It is not always easy and many times this increased awareness comes when we learn from our failures. It is an important skill to master.

If you want to take this a step further, you can also factor in the challenges to your *means* of communication: email, texting, social media posts, announcements, memos, etc. Written forms of communication present difficulty, because they lack the nuance of body language and tone of voice. Without watching a person's body language or hearing their tone of voice, written forms of communication allow your imagination to run wild. When you read something in all caps, you assume a certain tone. The same is true when you read something italicized or in bold print. You also read a message differently when it is accompanied by an exclamation point, or several.

Texting abbreviations also decrease effective communication. The result is an increased level of anxiety that leads to conflict. How many times have you stared at those bubbles that appear when someone is typing, waiting anxiously to see what they say? Alternatively, how anxious, or frustrated do you become when you know the message, email, or voicemail was delivered yet there is no response? Silence is also a means of communication, and sadly, it often increases conflict even further.

Since written communication allows for a wide range of interpretation by the reader, messages cannot always be effectively communicated through such means. I am not saying that certain messages are ineffective when communicated through various forms of technology. I am saying the use of these technological tools makes it more challenging.

A phone call can provide an avenue to effectively communicate your thoughts, but you may not always find a listening ear on the other end. You want to believe the other person realizes the importance of what you have to say. Yet, at the same time, you know that far too often people get distracted with their attempts to multi-task. They may set their smartphones on the desk or table, turn on the speaker,

> *The most effective way to communicate the importance of any message, directive, task, or urgent matter is face-to-face.*

and listen while they read and respond to email, surf the Internet, check out the latest on their social media pages, or complete other tasks.

The most effective way to communicate the importance of any message, directive, task, or urgent matter is face-to-face. Each military leader I interviewed highlighted the value of face-to-face communication. This approach is always better. A couple of critical things happen when you communicate one-on-one. First, it emphasizes the value of the person with whom you are communicating. Nothing says "I care about you" more than sitting down with someone to have a conversation, even if it is a difficult conversation. You have each other's undivided attention. Col. Dorminey explained that time is a leader's most valuable asset, and "to invest time with someone one-on-one sends a strong message about the importance you place on the individual." Second, the personal nature of this approach affords the individual an opportunity to ask questions. Asking questions lends greater clarification to anything that might have been misunderstood. Third, as the one delivering the message, you have an opportunity to ensure that what you think you are saying is what you actually say, because the other person has a chance to repeat what you've said, or they can ask clarifying questions. While I know this takes time and a lot more work, the approach ensures that resistance—or the conflict that accompanies it—can be minimized. And isn't this the goal of effective communication?

I realize that certain situations arise where face-to-face communication is not possible. When you *must* use other means of communication, work hard to ensure what and how you communicate is clear and concise. Use the most effective methods first, eliminating each one until you have exhausted the various means at your disposal. When face-to-face conversation is not possible, try the phone; if that is not possible, use an email or text message. Know the recipients of your communication and use the methods that reach them most effectively.

Operation

Daily operations tend to move according to the status quo. Most leaders prefer to operate without conflict and confrontation, and I understand the impulse. If everything moves along smoothly, everyone seems content. However, this can hinder the growth and development of your leadership and organization. Do your daily operations indicate a fixed mindset or one focused on growth? Carol Dweck's book, *Mindset,* will challenge you to consider these daily operations in relationship to how you think.[65] A fixed mindset is static: It avoids conflict, responds defensively, and is usually threatened by the success of others. On the other hand, a growth mindset is dynamic. It is constantly changing and adapting; it embraces conflict as an opportunity, persists when experiencing setbacks,

> *How you operate during conflict determines the desire, or the lack of desire, for others to follow your leadership.*

and is inspired by the success of others. The difference in these two mindsets is monumental. When you rethink how you operate, you must begin with an examination of your mindset. Is it a fixed mindset or a growth mindset?

How you operate during conflict impacts the desire, or the lack of desire, for others to follow your leadership. If you are content with standardizing operations without a willingness to adapt as product demands increase, work culture changes, and technology advances, people will eventually lose the desire to follow you. People hunger for growth and want to work in an environment where they not only thrive but excel.

You may have to step back and rethink how you operate and make necessary adjustments. Of course, when these adjustments are made, you know you must be prepared to deal with the resistance that follows from those who object. As much as one side wants change, the other side desires to keep everything operating the same. At this point, good negotiation skills are a starting point in navigating a positive flow to how you implement the needed changes to grow in your operations.

Negotiation

Few skills are more relevant and important than negotiation. In his book *Never Split the Difference,* former FBI negotiator Chris Voss explains that negotiating is part of daily life. He also claims that negotiation is simply communication with results. The central focus of the book is what he calls *Tactical Empathy.* Voss states, "It all starts with the universally applicable principle that people want to be understood and accepted. Listening is the cheapest, yet most effective concession we can make to get there. By listening intensely, a negotiator demonstrates empathy and shows a sincere desire to better understand what the other side is experiencing."[66] How you approach your negotiations determines the outcome. The skill of negotiation is designed to reach behavioral change. You are not looking for others just to agree with you, but to implement real life behavioral change. Voss indicates that the change begins with two words: "That's right."

He points out that moving people from where they are to where they need to be occurs with the use of effective pauses, minimal encouragement, mirroring, labeling emotions, paraphrasing, and summarizing the points of contention and their meaning. An effective discussion surfaces when you understand, pay attention, identify key emotions, and acknowledge those feelings. When done correctly, circumstances move in a positive direction for the negotiator. During discussions, when the one you are negotiating with admits "that's right," then you know they are taking a step in a direction toward behavioral change.

Voss claims, "There is no such thing as logical, only what matters to someone." He identifies three techniques to help with any negotiation. The first step is *tactical empathy*. People desire to be valued and understood. Negative emotions are present in any negotiation situation. Tactical empathy doesn't mean you agree with them but observe without reacting judgmentally. You acknowledge their emotions and recognize their perspective for the purpose of supplying positive input to reduce the intensity of the situation. The second technique involves *taking the sting out*. The idea here is to be preemptive. Address one's doubts or concerns by identifying the fears that may exist. Avoid allowing someone to move in the direction of assumptions, as it tends to allow negativity to creep into the situation. The third step is to *aim for fairness*. Fairness is quite subjective: After all, what is fair in the eyes of one person may not be the same in another. However, when something is seen as unfair feelings of disgust and aversion surface. The result is a lack of empathy, which leads to further conflict.

Situations occur in your work environment (discussing a raise, new position, vision, or strategic planning), in your home (financial responsibilities, purchasing a home, household labor, buying a car, disciplining children, helping with school assignments/sports/extracurricular activities, or setting curfew for teenagers), and in your community or religious organizations (helping those on the fringe, managing neighborhood watch programs, planning cleanup days, or supporting emotional, physical, spiritual efforts). These situations often create conflict. When this occurs, you need to know how to negotiate with everyone involved to help reach a positive and actionable outcome. You are not looking to compromise, but rather find common ground you can all agree on (getting everyone to admit, "that's right"). When this happens, you can move forward. Show people they matter (tactical empathy), demonstrate honesty (take the sting out), and be eager to find a solution without maliciousness (aim for fairness). These techniques will increase your ability to negotiate to a desired end.

As a final note, a friend and colleague shared this thought, "Silence is the most underestimated negotiating tool. It is rarely discussed, yet it is possibly the most important thing you can use." Learning to be silent, allowing the other person to think, process the discussion, and repeating what was heard provides an advantage when working toward the common ground of agreement.

Rethinking how you communicate, operate, and negotiate provides the first tactic for leading in the zones. Beginning with this tactic ensures a solid foundation by which each successive tactic continues to improve your ability to lead. The attention you give to ReCON will offer more opportunities to be rewarded as you move forward.

Tactic 2: Assess Resources

Before launching into any project in your strategy, you must be aware of the resources available to you. Certainly, any level of growth will require financial investment. How much is required will depend on the size and timeframe of the project. Before moving an organization out of the Comfort Zone into an initiated form of conflict, you should explore the financial costs involved. Determining the financial resources available ensures that you can overcome financial obstacles incurred along the way quickly, thus reducing the possibilities of economic setbacks and the conflict that often results.

You must also assess the material resources available to you. The nature of the task, mission, or project will determine the type of material resources needed. They may include structural materials (steel, concrete, wood, brick, etc.) or operational materials (office supplies, software, database, safety equipment, etc.). Take time to evaluate what materials are essential to begin and end the project, along with how readily accessible these materials are to you. Because these materials come at a cost, they factor into the financial resources required to complete the work.

Resources, however, involve far more than those of a financial or material nature. For example, emotional intelligence is an incredible, though often misunderstood, resource. You should assess the emotional intelligence you'll need to address the stress load that often accompanies the Combat Zone when change is introduced. Part of this process is to gain a better understanding of the emotional intelligence possessed by those who will be impacted by the proposed changes. Joshua Rosenthal with Talent Smart EQ points out that, "Emotional intelligence skills help us successfully navigate change in the same way they help us to be more effective at work and in life. What's more, emotional intelligence can help you not only manage change, but also to raise your awareness of how you and others typically think and behave when confronted with something new and unfamiliar."[67] Another source claims, "Leading transformational change needs leaders with the emotional intelligence to lead oneself amid organizational chaos and the agility to adapt within an ambiguous environment."[68]

To avoid drifting back into the Comfort Zone, or falling into the Danger Zone, you must be keenly aware of the emotional stress levels that can destroy momentum. When the load of stress increases, how will you react? How will others react? How will they feel in that moment? When tensions run high, you must know how to address them, even if that means finding counseling services, providing time away, or reducing the workload. However, as mentioned before, the most effective way to reduce tension while implementing change is through proactive, face-to-face communication.

When it comes to volunteer organizations, manpower is a critical resource to consider. Many civic organizations and churches rely heavily on a volunteer structure. While school systems employ administration, teachers, and coaches, they also rely on volunteers to assist at many levels. If you lead an organization reliant upon volunteers, it is essential to understand how to track the people willing to help and efficiently assign specific tasks required to complete a project. To do so, you will need to understand how many willing participants have volunteered, the skill level each volunteer possesses, their comfort level of working within specific tasks, and how much time each of them can commit to contributing to the project. Proper assessment of this resource can make a major impact on the direction of your organization.

When assessing the resources available or needed to accomplish any task, mission, or plan, calculate how much time is involved. Time is one of the most valuable, treasured, and essential commodities. Every level of the project you tackle will take time. The time you can dedicate to the work determines the amount of momentum you build as a team, the quantity and quality of the outcome, and the focus you establish as an organization for your vision. Once you assess the amount of time required, you can take steps toward implementing the plan.

Another key resource to consider is the creative abilities of the people who follow your leadership. I am constantly amazed at how untapped this resource is in many organizations. People abound with amazing talent, and their creativity, if unleashed, would probably shock you. When creativity is limited to only those in positions of leadership, organizations shackle one of their greatest resources. Encourage everyone to contribute their creativity to the development and implementation of every strategy, goal, and plan. When you do, you might just be surprised at the powerful results, and your organization will blossom.

When it comes to assessing resources, let me suggest a few ideas to help with the process.

Identify your needs or issues. Before the process of assessing resources begins, identify the needs or issues to be addressed. An awareness of the needs or issues is foundational for knowing the financial requirements, emotional intelligence, talent, time management, and creativity to move forward effectively. Be clear, explicit, and sure about the specifics of any need or issue. Clarity ensures the proper assessment of resources at every level.

Be realistic. To assess resources adequately, you must be realistic about each level described, especially the time requirements. How much time will be required to complete this project? Will you, your team, or organization have the amount of time required to finish well and provide a quality product?

Will the amount of time you dedicate to it be enough to meet the expectations of each objective within the project timeline?

Define obstacles or barriers. Any worthwhile project will face obstacles or barriers. The best way to overcome them is to prepare. I will talk more about preparing for resistance in the next tactic. For now, when you assess resources, take time to define anything and everything that might stand in the way of real success for you and your organization. Fulfilling this task will provide greater clarity for everyone.

Evaluate inconsistencies. An assessment of your resources will be incomplete without an evaluation of the gaps that exist. When you look back over the last one to five years, what changes would you make to improve the direction forward? Are there inconsistencies between conduct of operations and organizational values? Do not neglect or deny the inconsistencies that exist. Instead, work to make necessary changes that create alignment.

Ask for help. Whenever you reach a point that you are unwilling to ask for help, you can easily begin a downward spiral. The suggestion is best applied in the role of a mentor and mentee. Either individuals or a collective group, when you surround yourself with those who can guide and assist your leadership, everyone benefits. Other leaders have experienced the same or similar challenges as you. Seek their wisdom. Learn from their expertise. Getting an outside perspective often opens the door to greater opportunities for growth on a personal and professional level. The result translates into increased productivity for you and your organization.

You may think of additional ideas to assist you in assessing available resources. Once you know the needs or issues, assess necessary funding, personnel, time, and creative skills to succeed. This tactic will require change and change will bring resistance, so get ready.

Tactic 3: Prepare for Resistance

As I explained in Chapter 2, whenever change occurs, resistance raises its head. The nature of the resistance is directly affiliated with either forced or initiated conflict. Preparing for this resistance ahead of time will determine the long-term effects that follow.

A successful mission requires preparation. I remember finishing a presentation, which I thought was informative and delivered well. While greeting friends and family afterwards, an older gentleman walked up on my blind side and tapped me on the shoulder. When I turned around, he simply stated to me, "Bob, always remember the **5 Ps: Proper Preparation Prevents Poor Performance.**" Then, he just walked off. I was left standing there wondering if the presentation was that bad. Did it sound as if I was unprepared? I wasn't sure exactly how to interpret what I had just heard. In time, I began to realize the importance of what he told me, and it became an inside joke between us. When I moved to Colorado, he made sure to tell me that I needed to teach everyone the importance of the 5 Ps. The concept is as critical in leadership as it is in public speaking.

Many authors have dedicated books, articles, blogs, and journals to conflict resolution and the preparation required for it. Whether talking about family, friends, coworkers, neighbors, or fellow citizens in your community, conflict is part of life. You must deal with conflict almost daily, sometimes on a minor level and sometimes on a major level. Regardless of the relationship, even the slightest changes result in conflict. Since change occurs continually, you will find yourself frequently facing conflict.

Change represents one of many reasons why conflict exists today. How you navigate the turbulence that follows indicates the strength of your leadership. In their book, *Difficult Conversations: How to Discuss What Matters Most,* Douglas Stone, Bruce Patton, and Sheila Heen highlight three major questions that surface in conflict: What happened? How do I feel about it? And how will this impact me?[69] Your perception, emotions, and identity are wrapped up in these three questions. The last two are directly impacted by the first. When you feel your identity suffers or is attacked, conflict results. The following suggestions will help you prepare for conflict.

Anticipate conflict. Preparation begins with an anticipation of conflict. Several years ago, I attended a Chamber of Commerce banquet in Greenbrier, Arkansas. The guest speaker that night was former Arkansas governor Mike Huckabee. He referenced a conversation with an Olympian luge athlete, in which former governor Huckabee expressed how challenging the curves must be when traveling at high rates of speed. The athlete's response was simple: "You have to negotiate the curves before you get to them." The same is true of conflict: You need to anticipate conflict in advance and prepare for it. Far too many people wait until they are in the middle of the conflict to determine how to proceed. Imagine the difference when you are prepared for the conflict because you anticipated its arrival.

Ask the right questions. If not careful, we tend to listen to one side of a story and make assumptions or judgments about the entire situation. Remember that there are two sides to every story, and you should try to put yourself on the other side of the table to better understand the situation. The perception, emotions, and identity of each person involved will be unique. Closed-ended questions lead to information deficiency. Open-ended questions, however, allow for everyone involved to explain their perspective. These questions begin with words like "what, how, and why." What did you see? How did it make you feel? Why do you think this happened? A friend added two questions, "Why do you think/believe that?" and "What would it take to change your mind?" The questions may be modified depending on the situation, but asking the right questions promotes healthy dialogue between both sides of the conversation and opens the door for a clearer understanding.

Consider conflict as an opportunity, not a problem. If you only see conflict as a problem—an obstacle that prevents you from achieving success or happiness—then you do everything within your power to avoid it. While no one likes conflict, as a leader, you should recognize the value of conflict to challenge your thinking, enable growth, improve leadership ability, and strengthen relationships. This is not to suggest that you look for conflict, but you must recognize that carefully and methodically initiating conflict can help develop a more holistic approach to your leadership. Col. Dorminey told me, "Conflict is where things are happening. A lack of conflict is status quo at best and apathy at worst. As leaders we should want to be where things are happening to guide and influence the result. As such, we shouldn't be afraid of conflict, we should rush towards it. On the battlefield we refer to this as *move to the sound of gunfire*."

Practice the "101 Percent Principle."[70] Simply stated, this principle requires you to find the one percent you agree on with someone else and give one hundred percent of your effort to it. While it may seem counterintuitive on paper, many people tend to focus on disagreements before even looking for common ground. The result is greater conflict and division. How much better would it be if you found the areas of agreement and focused most of your attention there before you looked at the differences? This principle provides a place of psychological safety and comfort.[71]

Focus on one conflict at a time. You've heard the old saying, "Take one step at a time." This thought contains sage wisdom. When life hurls multiple challenges at you all at once, you can easily get overwhelmed. The result of these struggles can lead to discouragement and depression. How do you handle juggling multiple conflicts? The short answer is that you tackle one at a time. Ask yourself, "What must be done today? What problem must be resolved first?" If you focus on areas related to the future, your mind can be consumed with the specifics of what may be resolved in the future, and you fail to address the priority of today. If you address conflicts in order of necessity, you can knock them out in turn, creating a sort of mental domino effect.

Learn to listen. You must learn to listen. The ability to listen well is a lost art. My tendency is to think about how I will respond while the other person is talking. I listen long enough to get the idea and then wait for the person to draw breath so I can jump in and start sharing my thoughts. Learning to listen well involves the ability to repeat back a summary of what someone has said, as *you* understand it. This is referred to as *active listening*. You can use phrases like, "What I hear you saying is…" or "If I heard correctly, I understand you to have said…" Learning to listen in this way projects your desire to understand, and it provides the other person an opportunity to correct any misunderstanding. Another benefit of active listening is the ability to slow down and demonstrate a genuine care for the other person's perception, feelings, and identity. This is a win-win scenario.

Be willing to sacrifice *first*. This step is tough. We don't mind if someone else makes the sacrifice, but the personal application is costly. Instead of asking, "What kind of sacrifice will I *have* to make?", you should be asking, "Am I willing to make sacrifices? How much am I willing to sacrifice?" Resolving conflict for relational reconciliation is worth the sacrifice you make. If you are only concerned with what sacrifices you must make, you are more focused on checking boxes than developing relationships. When you approach your relationships with the willingness to make the sacrifice first, your humility stands out. Humility is a game-changer for resolving conflict. Pride will only push you into greater conflict and the Danger Zone, but humility increases your credibility. This contributes to resolution and strengthening relationships.

> When you approach your relationships with the willingness to make the sacrifice first, your humility stands out.

While this list is certainly not exhaustive, these ideas will help make a powerful impact on how you handle conflict when it arises. Consider them and add preparation methods specific to your personal situation.

Tactic 4: Communicate Effectively

Communication is the key concept of the fourth tactic, because effective leadership through the Combat Zone requires communicating who, what, when, where, and especially the why. Yes, I have already talked about effective communication. Now, let me clarify the difference between effective communication and communicating effectively. In Tactic 1, I referenced effective communication or rethinking your *means* of communication; this tactic is about implementation and understanding. The decision-making processes and communication in the armed forces are just as instructive to leadership in non-military contexts, and I drew upon several of these processes here.

Each branch of the armed forces uses a specific method when communicating the decision-making process. The Army uses a method referred to as the Military Decision-Making Process, which is a process in both tactical and garrison environments, combining collaborative planning, assessment, and preparation. The layout of this method follows certain protocol to guide each unit for making decisions in critical moments of combat and then communicating those decisions. The design increases understanding of the situation that contributes to the next step. According to Lightning Press, the process is "detailed, deliberate, and time-consuming."[72] Another procedure to communicate the mission is known as OSMEAC, formerly known as the Five Paragraph Order.[73] The details affiliated with each letter (Orientation, Situation, Mission, Execution, Administration / Logistics, and Command / Signal) lay out specifics within the communication process, and the description explains the thrust and purpose required to fulfill the mission.

Communication of these orders falls into two categories: Centralized communication (from the top down) and decentralized communication (from the bottom up). Once the communication has been received from the top, officers rely on a decentralized communication platform. The objective is given to each unit, but how they fulfill the objective is up to the unit within the perimeters of legal and ethical limits.

Communicating effectively during times of combat is crucial and potentially lifesaving. Lt. Col. Lewis made it clear that "communicating every step of the strategy is as critical as knowing the strategy itself." The strategy is established and communicated to each level of ranking officers down to every individual involved in carrying out the mission. Lewis explained that "to improve your ability to communicate effectively and reduce infractions along the way, due diligence is key." Leaders must communicate the formulation of the strategy and the involvement level of everyone required to fulfill the mission. You must communicate each step of the strategy as it unfolds, along with the steps that follow. Over-communicating has never been an issue when implementing plans for success. Under-communicating the plans or communicating them ineffectively, however, ensures frustration and conflict.

Why is all this emphasis upon communication important to leaders? Major Castaneda identified what he learned from a mentor, "If people are used to listening to you in garrison, whenever it gets to combat, they are so attuned to hearing your voice and command, they won't question it in combat." He continued to emphasize the significance of this thought: "If they

> *Followers need to hear your voice. Constantly communicating instills confidence in the entire organization.*

are used to your voice, because of the corrections you've made and communicated along the way, they know when you say something, they have confidence already that what you are telling them to do is the right thing to do, so they don't question it. They just act." Followers need to hear your voice. Constant communication instills confidence in the entire organization.

Another question I raised to these military leaders was, "How do you ensure what has been communicated is understood?" General Chaney used two practices: the Confirmation Brief and the Sand Table. He explained, "The Confirmation Brief involves communicating a strategy. I then give them time. Within a day or two, they must come back and brief me, explaining to me what I communicated to them." Most of the time, the briefing revealed aspects of miscues or misunderstanding. He then had the opportunity to clarify through two-way communication. He also explained the Sand Table: "Literally, we work on the ground. It is lines in the sand, mounds of dirt to represent mountains, all visual cues that others need to understand what you are trying to communicate." He noted that many carry a Sand Table Kit. This approach incorporates visual and collaborative planning to ensure the mission communicated is understood.

Captain Torian suggested what he called a push/pull system "where you push information out and people push information up to you. You can also use the pull system where you can set up a battle rhythm, i.e., you set up specific times to communicate at consistent intervals." He went on to explain his use of Commander Critical Information Requirements: "I want to hear from you if certain items or protocol happen or don't happen within the mission or objective. These are tailored to whatever the situation requires."

Vice Admiral Bucchi described an iterative process that involves verbal and written communications and daily meetings to work out details. He talked about the initial discussions in the planning stage of various scenarios that could potentially happen and what needs to be done in each. The plans and objectives are then explicitly written down and sent to each commander. Once each commander and his staff have the opportunity to look at the strategy, they respond by sending written questions for clarification. This document is then sent back up to leaders for a response. Admiral Bucchi also discussed what he called a "Drumbeat" in which commanders set aside a specific time each day for a video chat where everyone is given a chance to ensure all instructions, plans, and objectives were clear.

Colonel Dorminey explained the iterative process in the Space Force, "The plan only survives until first contact with the enemy. As such the plan won't get you very far in combat. You must be able to deviate from it quickly and efficiently to remain effective. It is the planning that allows this to happen. Military planning is iterative. The commander issues guidance and his/her staff develop courses of action that meet the intent of the guidance and brief those back to the commander. The commander modifies guidance, and the staff refines the courses of action. One course of action is eventually selected and refined through similar processes of iteration. In effect the planning process is a lengthy dialogue, between commander and staff, with constant guidance and feedback in both directions. Once the plan is complete everyone understands the objectives, the timing, the interdependencies and most importantly the *why*. The planning process ensures not only that the commander can be understood, but also that he cannot be misunderstood. As a result of all the *communication* in the planning process, the plan can be deviated from when required and still deliver the desired outcome. In this way, the plan is relatively meaningless, but planning process is everything. Communicating effectively is like the planning process. It is not a one directional or even a single event proposition. It is iterative through time."

Communication is about ***understanding***. Simply speaking the same language as someone else does not ensure that we have communicated effectively. The ability to speak a different language other than your native tongue is an incredible skill, but it does no good if your audience does not know the language. Leaders have a responsibility to know complex things yet possess the ability to explain them on a level their audience understands. If not, you might as well be speaking a different language. Moving your lips with audible sounds is not enough.

Major Castaneda referenced "Napoleon's Corporal," a common expression in the military. The idea simply means that if the lowest ranking military officer understands the command, you know it was communicated effectively. You must strive to clarify your guidance in a way that everyone understands. You want others to understand what you wish to express. This may require enough time to allow the other person to ask questions and repeat what they heard you communicate to them. Col. Dorminey clarified a transition in his career when it came to communicating to be understood. He said, "As I've matured in my leadership that thought has grown to 'communicate so you can NOT be misunderstood.' There is a difference, and it involves precise language and feedback to make sure the message sent was the one received." What this all means is you must consider the value of what and how you communicate.

The best communicators also know how to relate by using stories or illustrations. The ability to communicate information in story form or through an illustration, when relevant to the situation at hand, helps people remember. If you feel you do not have the creative talent to use story or illustration, then talk with someone on your team who is gifted in this area and get their help. In their book, *Made to Stick,*[74] Chip and Dan Heath provide a powerful resource for considering how to communicate in ways that connect and strengthen your ability to help people will remember.

The common denominator with these methods is a strong focus on understanding. Finding the right *means* and *method* of communication is essential for your leadership and the future of your family, community, church, or organization. Whether you implement a Confirmation Brief, Sand Table, push-pull, Drumbeat method, iterative planning, or make use of relevant stories to communicate, you must find what works most effectively for you as a leader and use it consistently.

Tactic 5: Engage in Mission-Training

The hyphen between these two words is intentional, because it represents an important way of thinking. Mission-training requires a knowledge of the mission *and* the essential training to carry out the mission. Is everyone involved aware of the mission and equipped to do their job, which is critical to the whole organization? Since everyone is essential to the overall mission, ensuring they fully understand the mission and are trained to do their part must not be overlooked. Understanding the mission involves communicating it effectively, as I discussed in the previous tactic. Equipping everyone to carry out the mission is the next step. General Chaney shared a common saying in the Army: "Hard training, easy war." His point was that "prior to combat, the more intense, realistic, and hard you can make the training, the more prepared you'll be when you get to war." He also emphasized the need to "stress everyone's skills." When you are placed in stressful and intense situations within a safe training environment, you will more likely operate well under the pressure of combat. Col. Dorminey quoted Richard Marcinko, Commander Seal Team Six, "The more you sweat in training the less you bleed in combat."

Vice Admiral Mike Bucchi outlined several steps in the Navy's mission-training process. It begins with what he called the "table-top" discussion, where military leaders examine pieces of the war picture and work through various scenarios. Second, he said teams go out to "execute exercises," where they begin with basic maneuvers and continue a process of layering stronger threats until they reach a high-intensity level of stress. The purpose is to "check the systems and [their] capabilities to respond to it." The final step he called the "debrief." He said, "The most important aspect of the whole flight was not the brief, not the actual execution in the air, but back in the red room." He explained how the entire team must methodically walk through the entire exercise to discuss what happened, what went well, and what did not go according to their plan. He also pointed out that leaders are required to evaluate and step back to make needed corrections.

General Chaney elaborated on the essential need for "rehearsals." In preparing for combat, the Army practices procedures prior to operations. He said, "Even the simple things you rehearse every single time. Prior to anyone hitting the ground, we spend the day before rehearsing, even if we have done it a hundred times before." He indicated that the rehearsals have value because they prevent complacency. One of the key areas he identified in this process involves the team understanding the intent of the operation. He said, "When they have been through the rehearsals, and understand the plan well enough—the part most leaders miss—you have to empower your team to make decisions and adjust on the fly." The reason for this is that no one ever knows one hundred percent of what will happen on the ground. General Chaney said, "The enemy does not act according to your plan. So, you have to be as prepared as possible to adjust." Empowering your team in this way builds trust, which improves communication. The more effective the communication, the greater success of the mission.

The Air Force uses what is called the "Red Flag" exercise. Col. Dorminey explained, "The Air Force instituted the Red Flag exercise partly in response to combat losses during Vietnam. The Air Force discovered that the survival rate of pilots who survive their first ten combat missions significantly increased. Red Flag is designed to give pilots those first ten "combat" missions in the form of an intense training exercise."

The realistic approach in this type of training affords every individual an opportunity to be tested in stressful situations. The intensity of these scenarios determines performance levels, which prepare you to face actual circumstances when dealing with conflict. These exercises surface your ability to handle stress and expose where weaknesses may exist. When trained for the mission, there is a greater likelihood of leading well under pressure.

As a leader, your knowledge of mission-training is invaluable. You must ensure followers know the mission *and* equip them with the specific skills related to the mission. For training to be truly effective, you must be connected to your followers. According to Lieutenant Colonel Lewis, the most important thing you can know or do as a leader is to "listen to those you lead and learn from them." It requires you to know the skill levels and abilities needed to carry out the mission, along with the skills and abilities of every person entrusted to your leadership. Only then can you elevate each person to reach their greatest potential and achieve the mission. Only then can you provide the essential training required to advance the mission.

> *You must ensure followers know the mission **and** equip them with the specific skills related to the mission. For training to be truly effective, you must be connected to followers.*

Tactic 6: Analyze

Analyzing your strategy before implementation can provide insurance against unanticipated disaster. Analyzing the strategy begins with those who are influential in carrying out the strategy. They must examine details and look for gaps. The second step is to bring in an outside source who can search for areas missed by the initial evaluation. The following questions will benefit the examination.

What was missed? Was every detail covered? When those who are influential and an outside source have an opportunity to evaluate the strategy, the chances of overlooking any gap are diminished. The result provides greater confidence in the direction.

Have you secured the resources needed to implement the strategy thoroughly? As I mentioned in a previous tactic, resources involve more than just funding. You certainly want to ensure the funds are secured, but also that the right talent is on board.

Do you have an adequate number of people in place to cover the work? One thing the pandemic taught us was the value of good personnel. Too few people can hinder an organization from achieving success.

What backup plan is in place if someone fails, misses a target date, or cannot perform the task? The expression, "Those who fail to plan, plan to fail," is a common and accurate thought in strategic planning. Part of the strategy must include a backup plan that addresses the risks involved in operational failure. Identifying these threats in advance will allow you to create a proactive risk mitigation strategy which will increase the efficacy of your preparation and reduce the possibility of a negative chain reaction.

What are similarly situated organizations doing to achieve this goal? As the saying goes, "There is nothing new under the sun." Others who have done or are currently involved in similar work should be consulted at some level. Comparing strategies helps reveal potential gaps that may need to be addressed.

After you've combed through your strategy searching for answers to these questions, look through all the details one more time. This added piece of insurance is worth the effort. The analysis tactic is the last one before execution. Again, the communication level at this phase of the plan challenges you to dig deeply. You want to ensure all the bases are covered before diving headlong into implementation. While this tactic can take a lot of time to complete, the outcome secures a greater level of long-term success for the organization. If an organization rushes through or skips this tactic, mistakes can be costly in reaching the End Zone. Take whatever time is necessary to analyze every "nook and cranny" of the strategy.

Tactic 7: Execute the Strategy

In this last tactical step, you finally implement your strategy. It is one of the most exciting in the process. To provide a perspective of how crucial this part of the strategy is, consider the words of James Clear, author of *Atomic Habits*: "If you are not working hard, ideas don't matter. The best idea is worthless without execution."[75] The most amazing vision and powerful mission are simply words on a piece of paper without execution.

If proper planning has been completed in developing your strategy, along with a thorough analysis of the strategy, then execution simply involves getting started. It is important to move to execution within a reasonable timeframe, so that you don't lose the momentum built during the previous tactics. Momentum creates a special force that drives an organization forward to the point of being unstoppable. John Maxwell refers to this as the "The Law of the Big Mo."[76] There is no substitute for it. When sports teams execute a game plan, the difference between winning and losing often revolves around momentum. The momentum can shift from one direction to another several times during any game. A turnover, a score, a good or bad play, silence or noise of the crowd, and motivational expressions from coaches or comrades can all factor into the shift in momentum.

> *Momentum creates a special force that drives an organization forward to the point of being unstoppable.*

When an organization begins the execution phase, it is time to find various ways to build momentum. Momentum can build for many reasons: maybe you reached a benchmark, made progress toward a goal, received positive feedback from clients, or provided encouragement at the managerial level. Once momentum builds, execution increases, and the organization excels. If momentum continues, impossibilities become possibilities.

As with planning your strategy, proper execution highlights an organization's performance level. Some organizations utilize a tiered communication strategy where senior leaders communicate to the next level down, which continues to each level below. When this strategy is practiced during business reviews, leaders know how to execute when it matters. At the execution level, it is crucial to ensure that every person knows where they are and what happens next. The more people know, the more efficiently they operate as a team.

Teamwork

A critical aspect of execution is facilitating teamwork and cooperation. The ability to interact and work effectively with others is a sign of emotional intelligence. Few qualities are needed more than EQ. The execution of an organization's strategy requires that everyone work together. At this stage, you must rely on your team. General Chaney said, "Trust your team and trust your preparation." He also pointed out that it all goes back to training: "You want to work out conflicts in hard training early. You work with your team to make them cohesive prior to deployment." Not only do you need to prepare as a leader, but you must prepare others involved to achieve progress. General Chaney went on to say, "The more cohesive and stronger the team is, the more conflicts will work themselves out as you move forward."

Cooperation among coworkers, among leaders, and between leaders and followers provides a smoother execution of the strategy. What does it take to ensure a high functioning team? Consider a few suggestions.

Unite everyone under the vision and mission. Teamwork does not happen if there is no vision and mission. These two components clearly and concisely communicated can ensure a high functioning team.

Model emotional intelligence. The ability to know one's own emotional responses to situations or "emotional regulation"[77] is one thing, but to recognize and know how to respond to the emotional responses of others is a key to efficient teamwork.

Establish goals and plans that are team centered. David Schwartz once said, "Goals are as essential to success as air is to life."[78] If you have no goals, it is amazing how you reach them with incredible accuracy. If you want to strengthen teamwork, ensure goals are in place. To ensure buy-in, involve the entire team in the planning process.

Give people hope. Napoleon is credited with saying, "Leaders are dealers in hope." When hope exists, teams come together and work hard. When there is hope, they will climb any mountain, walk through any valley, and overcome any obstacle. The power of hope—desire plus expectation—strengthens teams in their focus.

Address the terrorists. Once momentum starts building, the enemies of success enter the picture. The jealousy that occurs within teams is real. When this happens, leaders must address it quickly. Outside enemies also exist, and they work hard to prevent your organization from gaining momentum. Be kind, but firm. Have the courage to speak directly and not allow your team to suffer because of one or two people, especially those outside the organization. Leaders need the ability to adjust plans. Col. Dorminey said, "The plan won't survive first contact with the enemy because the enemy gets a vote. Whether the enemy is unforeseen obstacles or internal losses (a critical team member gets sick, etc.) the plan will have to alter. A leader must accept this reality and be prepared to adjust quickly and decisively without derailing the objectives."

Eliminate distractions. As momentum builds, so do distractions. Teams experience distractions in everything from failure to success. On one hand, a small setback can distract a team from focusing on the vision and mission. On the other hand, early successes can result in the same. Find ways to minimize and, if possible, eliminate distractions so everyone stays focused on the vision, mission, goals, and plans.

Practice the one-third two-thirds rule. Major Castaneda referred to this military practice in leadership. The basic application refers to leaders taking one-third of the time and responsibility when developing plans. Two-thirds of the responsibility is then delegated to the rest of the team to develop their own plans and execute them. The result is a high functioning team.

Lead by example. One of the greatest gifts you provide to your team is your example. You not only believe in the vision and mission, but you also show your confidence through your example in doing the work, walking alongside them.

As I have expressed, communication is key. Without it, success is only a dream or wish. Vision, mission, and strategic planning are building blocks for success. Any strategy requires the ability and means for communicating all three.

Debrief

Admiral Bucchi and Colonel Dorminey both referenced an essential need for the *debrief.* I've chosen to conclude this tactic emphasizing the debrief because of how it works with teams. Colonel Dorminey told me, "It is the key to failing forward." Ultimately, it leads to greater success. The debrief is designed to occur after the execution tactic since it is in the forefront of the team's mind. According to an article in Air Education and Training Command, "There is no rank in the debrief. The focus is to identify and communicate what happened, why it happened, discuss how we can do it better next time, and finally determine if we met our objectives. For the errors identified, do a root cause analysis." The author, Colonel Todd Dyer, went on to say, "The continual learning process is a tool we can all use to better our teams and ourselves."[80]

The playing field is level. All team members are equal. Teams have a chance for open and transparent discussion about the mission. Every detail of the mission, specifically failures, are deconstructed to determine ways to prevent them on future missions. Admiral Bucchi and Colonel Dorminey pointed to several benefits.

Evaluation. Admiral Bucchi clarified the debrief as a way to learn what worked and what did not. Teams evaluate what went well and should be repeated or what went poorly and needs to be adjusted. Here, they have the means to identify successes and failures. Errors require a root cause analysis. In his article, Colonel Dyer went on to write, "A root cause analysis is a deeper examination of the particular error, not just the first layer of the *onion*." Basically, the root cause analysis is a process of discovering the root cause of a problem, or error, with the intent of finding a solution.

Trust and accountability. Colonel Dorminey pointed out that teams learn a greater level of trust and accountability through this process. He said, "It requires honesty with the team as well as critical analysis. It is not easy, but the value is enormous." As details of the mission are brought to the table, teams have opportunity to discuss each member's contribution to the success or failure of the mission. The level of accountability increases, and the psychological safety experienced raises the level of trust between team members.

Planning and execution. The debrief improves future planning and execution. Colonel Dorminey said, "The debrief can be used at significant milestones and at the completion of the overall effort to great effect." What teams learn during the debrief provides a foundation for how to approach future missions. With a clear understanding of what did and did not work on previous missions, teams are better equipped to plan and execute future missions. Colonel Dyer also noted, "All players can now walk away from the debrief with a better understanding of how to improve planning for future events. Had the team not debriefed, critical errors identified during their discussion would be lost."

Leadership development. The result of the debrief provides any organization with an opportunity to develop leaders at all levels. Since there is no rank in the debrief, every team member develops skills to raise their leadership ability. From the airman first class to the colonel, everyone examines the details to discuss how to improve an approach to future missions.

The debrief is an essential tool for every team. The ability to evaluate details of the mission determining the root cause of failure and celebrating components that led to success strengthens every member of the team. Additionally, plans and execution for future missions improve. While leaders develop their ability to lead, ideally, the design of the debrief is to minimize and potentially eliminate future mistakes, ensuring greater success.

When you introduce the type of change that moves people out of their Comfort Zone, resistance follows. The level of resistance is directly affiliated with the type of conflict encountered. If it is forced conflict, expect stronger resistance. However, if you lay the proper groundwork, initiated conflict will minimize the level of resistance. Carefully leading through the Combat Zone can help you avoid returning to your Comfort Zone or diving into the Danger Zone. This strategy can carry you to the End Zone, where you can celebrate, evaluate, and motivate the entire organization. These seven tactics will guide you through each zone. Each is critical to the success you desire for your leadership and organization.

In The Zone – 7 Tactics

1. Now that you've read the 7 Tactics for Leading in the Zone, where would you place your leadership and organization, on a scale of 1 – 5.

   Needs work   1 —— 3 —— 5   Working well

2. What three suggestions would you give leaders to improve their ability to communicate the mission of the organization?

   a. _____

   b. _____

   c. _____

3. Share three ways your organization prepares for conflict.

   a. _____

   b. _____

   c. _____

4. What one suggestion would you give leaders to improve their ability to resolve conflict?

5. What is one major change that needs to be made in your organization?

6. How will you use these seven tactics to grow your leadership and strengthen your organization?

Scan the QR code below for a link to a worksheet that will help you implement the 7 Tactics of Leading the Zone.

Conclusion

The Road to Transformation

The journey of a thousand miles begins with a single step. The first step can begin the journey out of the Comfort Zone into an arena that projects you into a successful future. Taking the first step can be a daunting and fearful task. What happens if the conflict is too great? How will you react to the resistance? Do you really believe in the vision and mission of your organization? I wish I could tell you that the journey is easy, but it is not. Anyone who claims leadership is easy has never been a leader. Leadership means the road ahead will have hills and valleys, curves and straight stretches. There will be times when you can set the cruise control and times when you must have both hands on the wheel and a foot on the gas pedal. As with any journey, road construction must be completed to improve the drive, but in the meantime, it delays your travel plans. You must remain focused and aware to avoid moments when you will need to slam on the brakes. At times you will experience a flat tire. It is not a major bump in the road, but inconvenient all the same. Inclement weather can also create hazardous conditions for traveling. You will get tired. Yet, at other times you will feel invigorated at the opportunity to travel.

> *The challenges ahead of you can only be measured by the ability inside of you.*

Nothing feels better than seeing new and breath-taking scenery. Of course, reaching the destination fosters a sense of accomplishment. You made it. At the same time, you know you are here only for a short time, and you must get back on the road. Implementing the tactics discussed will help you keep your eyes on the road ahead and better prepare to avoid less than favorable driving conditions.

Make no mistake, traveling the road of leadership is no different. The challenges ahead of you can only be measured by the ability inside of you. The more you put into developing your leadership, the greater your ability to deal with the challenges you face. And the greater your ability to deal with those challenges, the more credibility you possess for people to follow. The time and energy you invest in your leadership make a difference for those who desire to follow a true and authentic leader. But regardless of where you are in your leadership journey, there are two guiding principles that should always keep you grounded: courage and character.

Courage

Leading from where you are to where you need to be will take courage. Most people tend to think of courage as a quality that people naturally possess. It is easy to begin thinking some people have it and others do not. In reality, courage is the result of making a decision to act bravely when you are scared to death. It is a skill that can be developed and strengthened. Everyone has some level of fear. Indeed, there are phobias of just about anything. There is even a phobia for fear: phobophobia![79] To summarize, people around the world are afraid of just about anything you can think of, and even the bravest people are scared of something.

After asking Vice Admiral Bucchi about the most important thing for a leader to know or do when facing a combat situation, he said, "You need to know yourself, know your people, and know the threat. A leader must be one who projects confidence and courage. They instill in people to be aggressive, but intelligently aggressive. They think outside of the box but are careful how far outside of the box they get. They are willing to take risk, but also line things up that will give them all the edge they can get." This is a perfect summary of the need for courage and the benefit it provides to leadership.

There seems to be a great need for courage, but if you only think of courage as a quality or characteristic, you will struggle to deal with your own fears. In his book, *Take the Stairs*, Rory Vaden talks about a woman trapped in a high rise building that was on fire. Her claustrophobia kept her from going down the stairwell and she was too high up to jump. Basically, she curled up under her desk and waited to die. When a firefighter found her, he attempted to take her down the stairs to safety, but she was resistant, fighting him. He finally whispered to her, "It is okay to be scared. Do it scared." He continued to reaffirm this all the way down the stairs until he brought her safely out of the building. This small phrase saved her life and transformed the way she approached other areas in her life where she experienced fear.[81]

Imagine the impact you would experience today if you faced your own fears the same way. The realization that it is okay to be scared can change the entire trajectory of an organization. Just remember to do it scared. Do not give up or abandon hope in the face of fear. Do not allow yourself to suffer from pride when it comes to acknowledging your fears. While few are willing to admit their fears, the ability to do so is the beginning of conquering them. When you do, fear is not eliminated, but it is addressed and overcome. This is courage.

> *While few are willing to admit their fears, the ability to do so is the beginning of conquering them.*

Character

The bedrock foundation of your leadership is character. I continue to appreciate the words of General Norman Schwarzkopf, "Leadership is the potent combination of strategy and character. If you must be without one, be without strategy."[82] His words remain as true today as when he first said them, more than fifty years ago.

What kind of character do you need to have to be effective? This is the sixty-four-million-dollar question. Think about the kind of character you want in a leader. If you develop those same qualities in your own life, there is a good chance others will follow, because they are looking for the same. Countless books have been written about character, so I will not exhaust the subject. However, I will share a few important notes about character for you to consider.

Develop integrity. How do you define integrity? I have asked this question several times and studied the subject at length. The most common response suggests that integrity is doing the right thing when no one else is watching, even when it costs you something or hurts. If you were to practice only this definition of integrity, everyone would notice the consistency that develops in your life. I remember a powerful thought shared by a friend, "Character is demonstrated in the difficult times, not in the easy. It's easy to have character when things are going well. The challenge is to have character in crisis. Integrity is one of the few things you really own. No one can take it away from you, but you can most certainly give it away."

Establish credibility. Defining credibility is a bit more challenging. It is closely associated with integrity and trust, with an exception. Technically, credibility refers to a quality of being trusted, believed in, convincing or believable. The process of gaining credibility sheds light on its definition. You gain credibility through your decision-making process. When you make good decisions, you strengthen your credibility.

Lead with honesty. Few qualities are more important in your leadership than being honest with others. This is foundational to other areas that make up your character. If you ever lie to people and they find out, you lose credibility, and they will not trust you or your leadership. The ability to be straightforward and honest with people builds stronger relationships. People will seek out your counsel if they know you will be honest with them.

Acquire humility. This trait can be confusing and misunderstood. Humility can be summarized by saying you do not think less of yourself, but you think of yourself less and of others more. When you work for the good of others, helping them reach their potential, and always consider the needs of others before your own, you will be recognized as possessing humility. When the opposite occurs, followers tend to view you as prideful, arrogant, or full of yourself. Developing humility is a life-long journey, but one that reaps great rewards.

Build trust. You have no greater commodity in your character than trust. People will not follow someone they do not trust. Once trust is broken in the relationship, it is nearly impossible to get back. As the saying goes, "It is easier to maintain than regain." Trust is usually built on the previous four traits I've discussed. If you want to be a great leader, then be trustworthy. When people trust you, they will go to the ends of the earth for you.

Courage and character are two indispensable components to your leadership. Develop them. Cherish them. Nurture them. When you do, your leadership will soar and the transformation that follows will be nothing short of life changing.

Intentional Transformation

Transforming your leadership is like building a bridge while you walk over it. Your ability to influence transformation in others requires you to constantly look forward to ways you can improve and strengthen your leadership.

Transformation suggests something is different; it is not the same as it was before. But transformation is something more than just difference. A slight change makes something "different," but when transformation occurs, the original is no longer recognizable. Transforming your leadership should resemble the metamorphosis a caterpillar undergoes to become a

> *Transformational leadership describes your ability to motivate and stimulate others to do more than is expected.*

butterfly. The result of the transformation makes the leadership better—much better. This transformation will make you different, but it will also spark a transformation in those who follow you.

Transformational leadership describes your ability to inspire others to do more than is expected. The intention is to help them grow in self-confidence in such a way that causes them to consider the needs of the organization and others before their own. It is kind of death and rebirth. When you grow in your ability to help others improve, you work on discontinuing indecisiveness, prejudice, small-mindedness, excuse-making, mental/emotional abuse, and poor communication. Transformational leaders influence the lives of all who follow. The ripple effect impacts every area of life.

Some of the greatest rewards one can reap from transformational leadership are idealized influence, inspirational motivation, individual consideration, and intellectual stimulation.[83] Idealized influence describes your ability to develop symbolic power used to influence others. Through a positive relationship, the follower develops an emotional attachment to the vision you cast. Inspirational motivation is a means of communicating a vision that is contrary to the status quo. Using symbols that focus on organizational effort makes the vision alluring. The idea involves looking to the future with creative ways to work within the guidelines of the organization. Individual consideration speaks to a mentoring role that responds to the needs and concerns of each follower while providing encouragement and support. You understand the self-efficacy of each person and tailor considerations better suited for a positive outcome for that person. Intellectual stimulation describes the efforts you make to overcome old problems in a new way. The enthusiasm you exude, while intellectually stimulating followers, also challenges them to question their preconceived ideas with out-of-the-box solutions.

Transformational leadership is a process, not an action or destination. Thus, transformation must be intentional. To be intentional means a decision must be made to do something about who and where you are as a leader, and to do so in such a way that positively impacts others. You cannot remain neutral or allow others to rest in the comforts of the status quo. You must be motivated in ways that move you and others into action, thus making something happen. The only way you improve is by being intentional. It does not happen by accident.

Leading in Your Zone

At a lecture I once attended, Ken Jones, former president of Lubbock Christian University, asked the question, "What is wisdom?" After a few seconds, he responded, "Wisdom is the space between black and white." You will often face the intimidating task of making decisions when there is no clear black and white answer. At that moment, you rely on wisdom to make the decision; but where does this wisdom come from and how do you come by it?

The answer can be complicated, primarily because wisdom is based on a foundation of knowledge and experience. Knowledge is acquired through several sources, such as studying, taking courses, or reading books. It can be gained by talking to and learning from others who have experience and expertise. Naturally, knowledge is also gained by your own personal experience, often referred to as the "school of hard knocks." The latter of the three can be the most challenging and difficult. It is certainly the most unpleasant. However, wisdom involves more than knowledge and experience.

Wisdom comes when your knowledge and experience inform your judgment. When your knowledge and experience are applied in your actions and decisions toward positive growth and development, you are gaining wisdom. Not every decision has a clear right and wrong solution. In these moments, you must use your knowledge and experience in application to the decisions you make.

I receive an email each week from James Clear, author of *Atomic Habits*. The thoughts each week challenge me to consider three ideas from him, two quotes from others, and one question for application. He shared this rich tidbit; "Knowledge is making the right choice *with* all the information. Wisdom is making the right choice *without* all the information" (emphasis mine).[84] The nature of this kind of wisdom is never more needed than in leadership.

The destination disease occurs when people feel they have reached the end, and there is nothing more to learn or accomplish. I appreciate something Col. Dorminey said, "If you believe this is the best it can get, you are correct because you will do nothing to make it better." This mindset quickly transitions organizations into the new Comfort Zone and if you are not careful the Danger Zone will soon be upon you as pride and arrogance are stirred up. The ability to lead people where they need to go while avoiding the destination disease is an essential skill and one that demonstrates wisdom.

As you near the end of this journey, I want you to think about where you are as a leader. Are you in the Comfort Zone, Combat Zone, Danger Zone, or End Zone? While it may sound odd, it is possible to experience all four zones at the same time. You may be leading a specific area that is still in the Comfort Zone, while in another area you are dealing with conflict in the Combat Zone. Furthermore, you may be facing challenges of the Danger Zone in parts of your organization while enjoying the End Zone in other areas. There is not always a rhyme or reason for when you face one zone or another. The secret to success is to recognize the characteristics of each zone and to lead through them carefully and tactically.

If you are still with me, then you have a pretty good idea which Zone you are dealing with or perhaps about to encounter. Regardless, it is up to you to recognize the challenges each Zone presents and learn how to lead people who follow you from where they are to where they need to go. The fact they have entrusted you with leading them speaks to your abilities. Use the opportunity to grow and learn how to improve your leadership and determine how you lead through challenges when they occur.

> *Too often, leaders make it **to** the end only to lose it **in** the end.*

Do not allow the End Zone to become the death of your organization. Too often, leaders make it *to* the end only to lose it *in* the end. You have the responsibility of preventing this from happening by leading powerfully. Focus on using the End Zone to be a life-giving opportunity to catapult your leadership and organization to a whole new level of success. While I refer to it as the End Zone, it is just the beginning—the beginning of something new, fresh, and exciting. Enjoy the opportunity to lead well.

Bringing Others Along

What do you want most as you lead through the winds of change? The legacy of your leadership will not be calculated in terms of dollars and cents. Nor will it be memorialized by buildings with your name on them. ***Your legacy will be measured by the number of people you brought along on the journey, equipping them to reach their greatest potential.*** Building relationships with every person entrusted to your leadership, motivating them to improve their abilities, and creating opportunities to collectively enjoy the rewards that come from a job well done, speaks to your legacy more than anything else.

Imagine a place where leaders not only welcome change but it is encouraged and supported.

Imagine the impact an organization can have if every person felt valued, heard, and appreciated for their abilities and contribution to the vision and mission.

Imagine the creativity that abounds if everyone is encouraged to provide insight toward the vision, mission, and accomplishment of organizational goals.

Imagine the quality and quantity of work that can be accomplished if everyone at every level is celebrated and rewarded for each step toward success.

Imagine the atmosphere of the workplace where everyone not only wants to come to work but loves being at work and feels inspired to be part of the organization.

Imagine the future of an organization where there are no limits placed on what can be accomplished.

Imagine the legacy you will leave if you navigate change with such a vision for the organization.

Just imagine.

References

1 Stevens, John. 2021. "The 4 Types of Leadership You Should Know." *Linkedin.* https://www.linkedin.com/pulse/4-types-leadership-you-should-know-john-stevens. Accessed 6 November 2021.

2 The Connected Generation. 2019. "Key Findings." *Barna Research Group.* https://theconnectedgeneration.com/key-findings/. Accessed 15 March 2020.

3 Ormand, Melanie. 2019. "A Mindset for the Road." https://www.roadbroads.com/tag/the-wealth-hike/. Accessed 4 June 2019.

4 Goff, Bob. 2020. *Dream Big: Know What You Want, Why You Want It, and What You're Going to Do About It.* Thomas Nelson Publishers: Nashville, TN.

5 Brown, Damon. 2011. "Beyond Borders: How the Failed Bookstore Chain Hastened Its Demise." *CBS News.* https://www.cbsnews.com/news/beyond-borders-how-the-failed-bookstore-chain-hastened-its-demise/. Accessed 6 April 2022.

6 Washington, Denzel. 2017. "Put God First." Dillard University Graduation Commencement. *Above Inspiration.* https://www.youtube.com/watch?v=2P_IKTPx9Ds&feature=share. Accessed 16 June 2020.

7 Turner, Chase. 2020. *T.R.I.A.L.S.: A Journey from Anxiety to Peace.* Springhill, TN: Kaio Publications.

8 Maxwell, John. 2014. "A New Definition of Success." https://www.johnmaxwell.com/blog/a-new-definition-of-success/. Accessed 3 March 2022.

9 Sull, Donald. 1999. "Why Good Companies Go Bad." Harvard Business Review. *Organizational Culture.* https://hbr.org/1999/07/why-good-companies-go-bad Accessed 5 April 2022.

10 Walsch, Neale. https://quotefancy.com/quote/872384/Neale-Donald-Walsch-Life-begin-at-the-end-of-your-Comfort-Zone-So-if-you-re-feeling. Accessed 2 February 2022.

11 The Connected Generation. 2019. "Key Findings." *Barna Research Group.* https://theconnectedgeneration.com/key-findings/. Accessed 20 April 2020.

12 Barnett, Megan. 2011. "IBM's Ginni Rometty: Growth and comfort do not coexist." *Fortune.* https://fortune.com/2011/10/05/ibms-ginni-rometty-growth-and-comfort-do-not-coexist/. Accessed 22 December 2022.

13 Kubicek, Jeremie and Steve Cockram. *100x Leader: How to Become Someone Worth Following.* Hoboken, New Jersey: John Wiley & Sons, Inc.

14 Maxwell, John. 2007. *21 Irrefutable Laws of Leadership: Follow Them and People will Follow You.* (10 Ed.) New York, NY: HarperCollins Leadership.

15 Graham, Gordon. Nd. "High Risk/Low Frequency Events in the Fire Service." https://www.youtube.com/watch?v=Og9Usv82CdU. Accessed 16 July 2022.

16 Marines. "Risk Management." MCO 5100.29.C Volume 2: Risk Management. https://www.safety.marines.mil/Risk-Management/. Accessed 21 December 2022.

17 Tolle, Echart. 2021. "Eckhart Tolle and the Coronavirus." *Electric Lemonade.* https://www.electriclemonade.com/eckhart-tolle-coronavirus/. Accessed 14 September 2022.

18 Mahoney, Ann I. 2014. "Senge, Covey, and Peters on Leadership Lessons." *Thompson Executive Leadership Institute.* https://schoolleadership.net/project/senge-covey-and-peters-on-leadership-lessons/. Accessed 4 April 2022.

19 Richards, Tony. 2016. *Life Focus: Leadership Keys for Life.* Parker, CO: Outskirts Press, Inc.

20 Marone, Mark. 2020. "The New Change Management: Leading Change in a VUCA World." *dalecarnegie.com.* Accessed 8 October 2022.

21 Stone, Charles. 2016. "8 Reasons Church Change is So Difficult." https://research.lifeway.com/2015/04/21/8-reasons-church-change-is-so-difficult/. Accessed 3 December 2021.

22 Gregory, Christina. 2021. "The Five Stages of Grief: An Examination of the Kübler-Ross Model." https://www.psycom.net/depression.central.grief.html. Accessed 19 November 2021.

23 Starr, Edwin. 1970. *War.* https://www.google.com/search?client=firefox-b-1-d&q=song+lyrics+for+war+by+edwin+starr. Accessed 19 April 2022.

24 Elmore, Tim. 2022. "Is It Possible to Assess Our Ability to Connect with Other Generations?" *Growing Leaders.* https://growingleaders.com/blog/is-it-possible-to-assess-our-ability-to-connect-with-other-generations/?mc_cid=c5a04e44d3&mc_eid=ea2a4f1ec7. Accessed 1 October 2022.

25 Voss, Chris. 2016. *Never Split the Difference: Negotiating as if Your Life Depended on It.* New York, NY: Harper Collins Publishers.

26 Wrigley, William Jr. *ForbesQuotes: Thoughts on the Business of Life.* https://www.forbes.com/quotes/author/william-wrigley-jr/. Accessed 19 April 2022.

27 Greenberg, Melanie. 2015. "The 3 Most Common Causes of Insecurity and How to Beat Them." Psychology Today. https://www.psychologytoday.com/us/blog/the-mindful-self-express/201512/the-3-most-common-causes-insecurity-and-how-beat-them. Accessed 19 June 2020.

28 Minow, Nell. 2020. "The Social Dilemma." *RogerEbert.com.* https://www.rogerebert.com/reviews/the-social-dilemma-movie-review-2020. Accessed 19 April 2022.

29 Clausewitz, Carl. "100 Von Clausewitz Quotes About War from The Prussian General." https://kidadl.com/articles/von-clausewitz-quotes-about-war-from-the-prussian-general. Accessed 4 March 2022.

30 Covey, Stephen M.R. 2018. *The Speed of Trust: The One Thing that Changes Everything.* New York, NY: Free Press.

31 Smith, Shelley. 2019. "Lack of Trust Can Make Workplaces Sick and Dysfunctional." *Forbes.* https://www.forbes.com/sites/forbescoachescouncil/2019/10/24/lack-of-trust-can-make-workplaces-sick-and-dysfunctional/?sh=f845df544d13. Accessed 14 April 2022.

32 Constable, Simon. 2021. "How the Enron Scandal Changed American Business Forever." *Time.* https://time.com/6125253/enron-scandal-changed-american-business-forever/. Accessed 14 April 2022.

<u>33</u> Hardy, Michael. 2015. "Watergate Scandal: Public Distrust of Government Begins." *Federal Times.* https://www.federaltimes.com/smr/50-years-federal-times/2015/12/01/watergate-scandal-public-distrust-of-government-begins/. Accessed 14 April 2022.

<u>34</u> Ziglar, Zig. "F.E.A.R." https://www.goodreads.com/quotes/976049-f-e-a-r-has-two-meanings-forget-everything-and-run-or-face. Accessed 20 November 2021.

<u>35</u> Carnegie, Dale. "Doubt and Fear." https://www.brainyquote.com/quotes/dale_carnegie_132157. Accessed 20 November 2021.

<u>36</u> Pagonis. William G. 1992. *Moving Mountains: Lessons in Leadership and Logistics from the Gulf War.* Boston, MA: Harvard Business School Press.

<u>37</u> Tzu, Sun, translated by Ralph D. Sawyer. 1994. *The Art of War.* New York, NY: Basic Books.

<u>38</u> Godin, Seth. 2022. "How Change Happens." *Seth's Blog.* https://seths.blog/2022/05/how-change-happens/. Accessed 31 May 2022.

<u>39</u> Covey, Stephen. 2020. *7 Habits of Highly Effective People: Powerful Lessons for Personal Change.* New York, NY: Simon & Schuster

<u>40</u> Goldin, Kara. 2018. "Great Leaders Take People Where They May Not Want To Go." *ForbesWomen.* https://www.forbes.com/sites/karagoldin/2018/10/01/great-leaders-take-people-where-they-may-not-want-to-go/?sh=167a1bdc1421. Accessed 20 February 2022.

<u>41</u> Indeed Editorial Team. 2021. "Centralized vs. Decentralized Structures: Key Differences." *Indeed.* https://www.indeed.com/career-advice/career-development/centralized-vs-decentralized. Accessed 22 December 2022.

<u>42</u> "The Decision Matrix: How to Prioritize What Matters." *Farnam Street Media.* https://fs.blog/decision-matrix/. Accessed 14 April 2022.

<u>43</u> Malhotra, Sanjay. 2018. "4 Styles of Decision-Making: A Leader's Guide. *The Enterprisers Project.* https://enterprisersproject.com/article/2018/7/4-styles-decision-making-leaders-guide?page=0%2C1. Accessed 14 April 2022.

<u>44</u> Drucker, Peter F. 1967. "The Effective Decision." *Harvard Business Review.* https://hbr.org/1967/01/the-effective-decision. Accessed 14 April 2022.

<u>45</u> Zyl, Ebben Van, Andrew Campbell, and Liezel Lues. (Eds.). 2020. *Chaos is a Gift? Leading Oneself in Uncertain and Complex Environments.* Republic of South Africa, Randburg: KR Publishing.

<u>46</u> Loggins, Kenny. 1986. "Danger Zone." https://www.google.com/search?client=firefox-b-1-d&q=kenny+loggins+danger+zone+lyrics. Accessed 20 November 2021.

<u>47</u> Dickerson, Doug. 2019 "How to Defeat a Culture of Apathy." *Doug Dickerson on Leadership.* https://www.dougdickerson.net/2019/05/12/how-to-defeat-a-culture-of-apathy/. Accessed 6 January 2022.

<u>48</u> Mayo Clinic Staff. 2022. "Positive Thinking: Stop Negative Self-Talk to Reduce Stress." *Mayo Clinic Healthy Lifestyle: Stress Management.* https://www.mayoclinic.org/healthy-lifestyle/stress-management/in-depth/positive-thinking/art-20043950. Accessed 18 April 2022.

<u>49</u> Gladwell, Malcolm. 2013. *David and Goliath: Underdogs, Misfits, and the Art of Battling Giants.* New York, NY: Little, Brown and Company Hachette Book Group.

<u>50</u> Navarro, Joe. 2021. *Be Exceptional: Master the Five Traits that Set Extraordinary People Apart.* New York, NY: HarperCollins Publishers.

<u>51</u> Edmundson, Amy. 2018. *The Fearless Organization: Creating Psychological Safety in the Workplace for Learning, Innovation, and Growth.* Hoboken, New Jersey: John Wiley & Sons, Inc. Publishers.

<u>52</u> Lake, Mac. 2020. *The Multiplication Effect: Building a Leadership Pipeline that Solves Your Leadership Shortage.* Nashville, TN: Thomas Nelson Publishers.

<u>53</u> Time Management. 2018. "Time Management Matrix". *Week Plan.* https://weekplan.net/academy/weekly planning/4-quadrants-of-time-management. Accessed 22 February 2022.

<u>54</u> Sinek, Simon. 2009. *Start with Why: How Great Leaders Inspired Everyone To Take Action.* New York, NY: Penguin Group.

<u>55</u> Miller, Dave. 2008. "Jim McKay: The Thrill of Victory…The Agony of Defeat." *BleacherReport.* https://bleacherreport.com/articles/29612-jim-mckay-the-thrill-of-victorythe-agony-of-defeat. Accessed 5 June 2022.

<u>56</u> Reid, Fabian. 2022. "The Power of Your Inner Vision." An excerpt *Your Time is Now*. https://fabianreid.com/wp-content/uploads/2018/01/The-Power-of-Your-Inner-Vision.pdf. Accessed 3 February 2022.

<u>57</u> Picchi, Aimee. "Here's a Top Reason Americans are Carrying an Average Credit Card Balance of Over $6,200." *USA Today*. https://www.usatoday.com/story/money/2020/02/12/credit-card-debt-average-balance-hits-6-200-and-limit-31-000/4722897002/. Accessed 19 January 2021.

<u>58</u> Reichert, Jack. 2018. "Make Yourself Dispensable." *Forbes*. https://www.forbes.com/sites/forbestechcouncil/2018/02/21/make-yourself-dispensable/?sh=508bc7fb674d. Accessed February 11 2021.

<u>59</u> Stanley, Andy. 2007. *Making Vision Stick*. Grand Rapids, Michigan: Zondervan Publishing Company.

<u>60</u> Hopkins, Tom. 2012. *Boot Camp Sales Mastery*. Tom Hopkins International.

<u>61</u> Duckworth, Angela. 2016. *GRIT: The Power of Passion and Perseverance*. New York, NY: Scribner.

<u>62</u> Dsouza, Maxim. "OODA Loop–How To Make Better Decisions In 4 Steps." *Productive Club*. https://productiveclub.com/ooda-loop/. Accessed 5 August 2022.

<u>63</u> McKay, Brett and Kay. 2021. "The Tao of Boyd: How to Master the OODA Loop." *The Art of Manliness*. https://www.artofmanliness.com/character/behavior/ooda-loop/. Accessed 5 August 2022.

<u>64</u> Arbinger Institute. 2018. *Leadership and Self-Deception: Getting Out of the Box*. Oakland, CA: Berrett-Koehler Publishers, Inc.

___ Arbinger Institute. 2006. *The Anatomy of Peace: Resolving the Heart of Conflict*. Oakland, CA: Berrett-Koehler Publishers, Inc.

___ Arbinger Institute. 2019. *The Outward Mindset: How to Change Lives and Transform Organizations*. Oakland, CA: Berrett-Koehler Publishers, Inc.

<u>65</u> Dweck, Carol. 2006. *Mindset: The New Psychology of Success*. New York, NY. Random House.

<u>66</u> Voss, Chris. 2016. *Never Split the Difference: Negotiating as if Your Life Depended on It*. New York, NY: Harper Collins Publishers.

<u>67</u> Rosenthal, Joshua. 2022. "An Emotionally Intelligent Change Model." *TalentSmartEQ*. https://www.talentsmarteq.com/blog/an-emotionally-intelligent-change-model/. Accessed 19 July 2022.

<u>68</u> Zyl, Ebben Van, Andrew Campbell, and Liezel Lues. (Eds.). 2020. *Chaos is a Gift? Leading Oneself in Uncertain and Complex Environments*. Republic of South Africa, Randburg: KR Publishing.

<u>69</u> Stone, Douglas, Bruce Patton, and Sheila Heen. 1999. *Difficult Conversations: How to Discuss What Matters Most*. New York, NY: Penguin Books.

<u>70</u> Johnson, Liz. 2009. "Realizing the 101 Percent Principle." *Ezine Articles*. https://ezinearticles.com/?Realizing-the-101-Percent-Principle&id=2511971. Accessed 2 February 2022.

<u>71</u> Navarro, Joe. 2021. *Be Exceptional: Master the Five Traits that Set Extraordinary People Apart*. New York, NY: HarperCollins Publishers.

<u>72</u> MDMP. 2022. "About the Military Decision-making Process [MDMP]. *The Lightning Press.* https://www.thelightningpress.com/about-the-military-decisionmaking-process-mdmp/. Accessed 6 February 2022.

<u>73</u> Boshard, Andrew. 2019. "OSMEAC." *Medium.* https://medium.com/@chaseboshard/osmeac-469392e06faf. Accessed 22 December 2022.

<u>74</u> Heath, Chip and Dan. 2007. *Made to Stick: Why Some Ideas Survive and Others Die*. New York, NY: Penguin Random House Publishers.

<u>75</u> Clear, James. 2018. *Atomic Habits: An Easy & Proven Way to Build Good Habits & Break Bad Ones*. New York, NY. Penguin Random House Publishers.

<u>76</u> Maxwell, John. 2007. *21 Irrefutable Laws of Leadership: Follow Them and People will Follow You*. (10 Ed.) New York, NY: HarperCollins Leadership.

<u>77</u> Navarro, Joe. 2021. *Be Exceptional: Master the Five Traits that Set Extraordinary People Apart*. New York, NY: HarperCollins Publishers.

<u>78</u> Schwartz, David. 1965. *Magic of Thinking Big: Acquire the Secrets of Success...Achieve Everything You've Always Wanted*. New York, NY: Simon & Schuster Publishers.

<u>79</u> Olesen, Jacob. 2022 "Fear of Fear Phobia – Phobophobia." *Fearof.net: The Ultimate List of Phobias and Fears.* https://www.fearof.net/fear-of-fear-phobia-phobophobia/. Accessed 10 April 2022.

80 Dyer, Todd. 2019. "The Art of the Debrief." *Air Education and Command.* https://www.aetc.af.mil/News/Article-Display/Article/1917581/the-art-of-the-debrief/. Accessed 31 December 2022.

81 Vaden, Rory. 2012. *Take the Stairs: 7 Steps to Achieving True Success.* New York, NY. Penguin Group.

82 Coetsee, Dirk. 2017. "Leadership: A Potent Combination of Strategy and Character. *ExpertHub.* https://www.experthub.info/business/strategy/leadership-a-potent-combination-of-strategy-and-character/?amp. Accessed 11 November 2021.

83 Farnsworth, Derek, Jennifer L. Clark, John Hall, Shannon Johnson, Allen Wysocki, and Karl Kepner. 2020. "Transformational Leadership: The Transformation of Managers and Associates." *IFAS Extension University of Florida.* https://edis.ifas.ufl.edu/publication/HR020. Accessed 8 June 2022.

84 Clear, James. "3-2-1: Knowledge vs. Wisdom, the time to worry, and how to encourage curiosity." https://www.jamesclear.com. Accessed 14 July 2022.

Printed in the USA
CPSIA information can be obtained
at www.ICGtesting.com
JSHW012044030823
45865JS00004B/23